D0089594

Women of Influence, Women of Vision

A Cross-Generational Study
of Leaders and Social Change

Helen S. Astin
Carole Leland

Foreword by
Charlotte Bunch

WOMEN of INFLUENCE, WOMEN of VISION

A Cross-Generational Study of Leaders and Social Change

 Jossey-Bass Publishers
San Francisco

Copyright © 1991 by Jossey-Bass Inc., Publishers, 350 Sansome Street, San Francisco, California 94104.

FIRST PAPERBACK EDITION PUBLISHED IN 1999.

All rights reserved. No part of this publication may be reproduced, stored in a retrieval system, or transmitted, in any form or by any means, electronic, mechanical, photocopying, recording, or otherwise, without the prior written permission of the publisher.

Jossey-Bass books and products are available through most bookstores. To contact Jossey-Bass directly, call (888) 378-2537, fax to (800) 605-2665, or visit our website at www.josseybass.com.

Substantial discounts on bulk quantities of Jossey-Bass books are available to corporations, professional associations, and other organizations. For details and discount information, contact the special sales department at Jossey-Bass.

Manufactured in the United States of America

Library of Congress Cataloging-in-Publication Data
Astin, Helen S., date.
    Women of influence, women of vision : a cross-generational study of leaders and social change / Helen S. Astin, Carole Leland.
        p.   cm.—(The Jossey-Bass social and behavioral science series) (The Jossey-Bass higher and adult education series)
    Includes bibliographical references and index.
    ISBN 1-55542-357-4
    ISBN 0-7879-5221-4 (paperback)
    1. Women in public life—United States. 2. Leadership. 3. Women social reformers—United States. 4. Feminism—United States. 5. Women—United States—Social conditions. I. Leland, Carole, date. II. Title. III. Series. IV. Series: The Jossey-Bass higher and adult education series.
HQ1391.U5A87   1991
305.42'0973—dc20   91-10784

FIRST EDITION
HB Printing   10 9 8 7 6 5 4
PB Printing   10 9 8 7 6 5 4 3 2 1

A joint publication in

The Jossey-Bass
Social and Behavioral Science Series

and

The Jossey-Bass
Higher and Adult Education Series

CONTENTS

FOREWORD

During the past three decades, women have taken a leadership role in redefining fundamental aspects of our lives—work, family, sexuality, equality, and justice. Women have influenced how we define reality, conceive of knowledge, and exercise leadership. This has happened both through the collective leadership of women as a social force and through the efforts of many individual women giving shape to this movement in its diverse forms. Clearly, women have achieved tremendous changes in this time; yet there are few studies of the women leaders who made this happen and of how they did so. What research exists rarely goes beyond the most visible spokeswomen, and little is known of the creative approaches to leadership that have been at the heart of this movement. This book helps to fill that gap with its focus on three generations of women leaders who have successfully worked for change in education and public service.

Helen S. Astin and Carole Leland take us beyond conventional views of leadership by looking not so much at the official positions of leaders but rather at what these women achieved and how they did it. They take us into a more complex and thoughtful exploration of diverse women's efforts to lead through empowering others and enabling groups to take action. They also reveal the fallacy of assuming that because women are still too few in number in public positions of power they have not been leaders in various efforts at change. By exploring the gains these women have achieved through leadership and what has motivated them to become leaders, we acquire a more complete picture of women's enormous collective leadership for change during this period.

While examining how these women have led, the authors avoid the pitfall of labeling certain traits "female" and instead focus concretely on what committed women leaders have achieved and what has been its impact. Thus, they not only shed light on women's specific leadership experience but also point to models for empowering leadership that are applicable generally. This is much richer, more provocative, and more useful material than the debate over whether there are innately female leadership styles. For that is not really the right question. It is more important to ask why there has been so little attention paid to women leaders over the years as well as why the styles of leading more often exhibited by women are particularly useful at this critical moment in history.

The empowering, cooperative approaches most often associated with women are not exclusively female terrain. If we see these as crucial models for leadership in the twenty-first century, then we do not want only women to adopt them. On the contrary, it is important to break down the mind-set that labels such behavior "feminine," serving to stigmatize it as weak, or less desirable than real leadership, especially at the highest echelons of patriarchal power. It is precisely in such places that female leaders and new approaches are most desperately needed if we are to change the patterns of domination that have become so destructive to the world.

Central to domination is the idea that where there is difference, then one group or approach must be superior and dominate the others: leaders over followers, men over women, whites over blacks, heterosexuals over homosexuals, one religion or nation over another, and so on. The wars, violence, and pillage of nature that have resulted from this hierarchical domination model now threaten the very existence of our planet. As a people we must find a more cooperative partnership approach to relations among us and with the earth; in so doing, we need leadership that is also cooperative and not based on the domination model.

In this search for new leadership forms, it is useful to see cooperative, empowering models not as inherently female but as female-led. That is to say, these approaches have been exercised by women more often than by men because they spring from the socialization of women as nurturers and sustainers of life. Thus women who have often practiced and developed them are now in a good position to assume leadership in teaching their usefulness to a society that must shift toward cooperation and away from hierarchy. As our culture seeks more appropriate styles of leadership in the future, studies of how women have led in varying circumstances will serve us well.

This book also ventures into the realm of women's history recording. The leaders in this study and others like them are too often overlooked by the "great man" approach to history. Women's leadership in civic and community affairs has long played an important role in the United States but has not been acknowledged, much less deemed important. In many ways, then, the women's leadership approaches recorded here are not entirely new. Rather, they are newly acknowledged and valued styles that have gained more acceptance as women's leadership has become more apparent over the past two decades. Women's leadership has grown both in numbers of public figures and in its visibility as all aspects of women's lives have been made more manifest by the women's movement in both politics and scholarship.

Women's leadership in education and community service has been vital throughout this century. Reading this book reminded me of the leadership empowerment that I received as a college student in the early 1960s from both black and white women active in the civil rights movement in the South. While black male leaders were the ones whom the press called on to be the spokesmen, it was often the black women who made things happen, especially in terms of organizing people at the community level before the white male press became interested in civil rights. Theirs was an empowering model that inspired younger women like me (many of whom later became feminists), even when we were not conscious of it as "leadership." Belatedly, this black female leadership of the most formative U.S. social movement in the second half of this century is finally beginning to be acknowledged, recorded, and analyzed. So too women's leadership in other areas of our society has barely begun to be visible, and books like this one point to the richness of female leadership experience needing to be explored.

Astin and Leland have shaped a fitting tribute to the legacy of the seventy-seven women leaders they interviewed. By documenting their leadership and why they were so passionate in their quest for social justice, they have furthered that quest and provided us with insights into the nature of cooperative leadership. They have left a visible record not only of these individual women but also of the collective consciousness that they were both a part of and fostered in others. It is the record of a vision of leadership for the future that strengthens those already engaged in seeking a more cooperative and sustainable world and empowers others to imagine such a possibility and to join in the effort to realize that vision.

New Brunswick, New Jersey   Charlotte Bunch
June 1991   *Director, Center for Global Issues*
                                                    and Women's Leadership
                                                        Douglass College
                                                       Rutgers University

PREFACE

We met almost thirty years ago on the Stanford University campus—a researcher completing a major monograph on women and an administrator finishing her doctorate. From that time until the present, we have remained close personal friends and professional colleagues. We have continued to support each other in our professional growth and to share many of the triumphs and tensions of our personal and professional lives. Throughout the years, two major themes have provided our common bonds and prompted continuous dialogue—*women* and *leadership*.

Leadership, of course, has been a popular, sometimes urgent, theme in the thoughts and writings of many other women and men during the past decade. In spite of voluminous anecdotal and scholarly work on the subject, however, leadership remains an elusive and perplexing phenomenon. We share John Gardner's conclusion that "the conventional views of leadership are shallow and set us up for endless disappointment" (1990, p. xi).

Being dissatisfied with the "conventional views," we looked for new cues and opportunities. In the early 1980s, we heard people beginning to discuss leadership in terms with which we resonated— vision, personal commitment, empowerment, and risk. This was in part the language of the modern women's movement. We realized that the period of social change we had been witnessing and participating in offered us leadership by women and for women as a model of leadership for social change. Our in-depth study of seventy-seven women focuses on these "instigators" as well as on some of the women leaders who preceded and followed them. These women had a passion for justice and equality that propelled the remarkable achievements chronicled here and offered the inspiration for our book.

The Study

In 1983 we invited a group of women leaders from diverse fields to meet with us to share their observations about the impact of the women's movement on the lives of women. During our three days of discussion at the Wingspread Conference Center in Racine, Wisconsin, the group reflected on a number of issues affecting women. Among the topics discussed were the progress of the women's movement and the identification of needs and possible strategies for the future. These critical deliberations at Wingspread provided us with the conceptual framework we needed to design and undertake the present study. In addition to helping us identify leadership issues that needed further exploration, the conference convinced us that the experiences of women leaders could be of substantial value in helping us understand not only what leadership means but also what constitutes effective leadership for social change.

We began our study in 1984 with three primary goals:

1. *To profile and compare women who provided leadership during the first two decades of the modern women's movement in the United States, roughly from the mid 1960s to the mid 1980s.* The group of women in this leadership study we called *Instigators* were women who were visible change agents and who are recognized for their significant accomplishments on behalf of women. Some Instigators associated with specific organizations, institutions, or coalitions we called *positional* leaders; others, identified as leaders because of their influence and leadership as academic scholars and teachers, we called *nonpositional* leaders.

We considered it essential to include two other cohorts of women leaders in order to enhance our understanding of the social and historical context of leadership, and to explore some aspects of leadership succession. To our Instigators, therefore, we added a representative group of *Predecessors*, women who served in leadership roles—primarily as institutional administrators—during the 1940s and 1950s; and a cohort of *Inheritors*, women who began to assume leadership roles during the second decade of the modern women's movement.

2. *To document the experiences, perspectives, and accomplishments of the three groups of women leaders during these decades.* Although new women's organizations, legislation, research, and writing developed in the 1960s and 1970s, the actual events—the struggles and the successes—have not often been recorded or reported. Many Americans have a general notion of what the modern women's movement is about, but few know the specifics as viewed through the eyes of the women who played major leadership roles.

3. *To develop a conceptual model for future studies of leadership derived from the experience of leaders in this study.* By focusing on such leadership dimensions as style, strategy, influence, power, and interpersonal relationships, we hoped to contribute both theoretically and practically to the study and practice of leadership.

The Book

This book is about women leaders and a social movement—the modern women's movement. It is about leadership within the context of education, broadly defined: colleges and universities, foundations, national educational organizations, and other public service agencies. While the book is limited to education, we hope that what is learned about women as leaders will inform and enlarge our understanding of leadership. The personal recollections and stories of the women we studied provide significant illustrations of a kind of leadership that is nonhierarchical and collective. We witness through them the passion, the vision, and the personal commitment that have helped us formulate a unique perspective on leaders and leadership. And they remind us that leadership involves a diversity of effective styles, strategies, risks, and initiatives.

This is also a book about legacies. It reminds us that the

accomplishments of the early 1960s were far-reaching, especially in matters of equity and inclusion. In many ways, the study is a personalized history of the struggles that brought about opportunities that many of us now enjoy.

Equally important, we acknowledge what the book does not offer. First, we were not able to include the perspectives of many other women leaders who played key roles as Instigators. Many of them were either unavailable or simply out of our reach within the limits of time, money, and geography imposed on our study. Second, while we tried to identify the critical events and outcomes that characterize this period of social activism—especially those directly linked with our seventy-seven leaders—we almost certainly missed some of the important historical events and issues.

Two other points deserve special note. This is not a comparative study of women and men leaders that focuses on gender differences. We value the contributions of comparative works, but, in the interest of understanding leadership and the women's movement, we find our focus on women appropriate and particularly important. We believe that an examination of the "what" and "how" of leadership as portrayed by these women will enable us to think about leaders in a way that will be fruitful to the study and practice of leadership generally.

Finally, this is a descriptive study, not a prescriptive one. It does not tell someone how to become a leader. Our hope is that the personal accounts and commentaries selected from hundreds of pages of interview transcripts will inspire others as they have us, and that they will stimulate more research and writing in greater depth and detail about women and about leaders. Above all, we hope the book will remind us all of the enormous legacy these women have provided and will kindle or rekindle in each of us our own passions and visions on behalf of women and society.

Audience

The book is intended for readers interested in the study and practice of leadership. It will also be of interest to certain specific groups: academic researchers and practitioners, feminist scholars and activists, and those interested in diversity issues and human resource development.

Overview of the Contents

The book comprises nine chapters. Chapter One provides the context for this study. We discuss the nature of leadership in general and present a conceptual model that serves as the organizing framework for the study. This chapter also provides an outline of the method and process of data collection.

Chapter Two provides a description of the social and historical context. It describes the issues and concerns of the second wave of the women's movement and portrays some of the generational differences of the women in the study, which often are the result of historical imperatives.

Chapter Three describes the formative influences on the women leaders. It looks at the family backgrounds, at mentors and role models, and at key experiences during the early years of schooling, during college, and in work and community activities.

Chapter Four provides an understanding of the forces that shaped the women leaders' commitment to social justice and involvement in leadership activities. It examines their vision and values and the personal dynamics that moved them into action on behalf of women.

Chapter Five describes the outcomes of their leadership efforts—initiatives within the academic community, educational organizations, publications and journals, and legislation and national policy. The chapter also analyzes the triggering events that led to these initiatives and changes.

Chapter Six focuses on the dynamics of leadership. It examines the special skills and strategies for change and it uncovers some of the elements in empowerment. Women leaders describe the critical nature of networks, collective action, and capacity for self-analysis.

Chapter Seven looks at the costs of leadership: what are the challenges, obstacles, and pains that these leaders experienced and how do they manage to overcome them? It also looks at the ways women leaders replenish themselves.

Chapter Eight reviews the accomplishments of the second wave of the women's movement—accomplishments that in large part are the result of the leadership provided by the women in the study during the early years of the movement. The analysis of these issues and accomplishments is that provided by the study's participants themselves, who also talk about a future feminist agenda.

Chapter Nine provides a summary of our major findings and suggests implications for the study and practice of leadership. In outlining future directions, we provide recommendations for further research studies and suggest ways to contribute to the development of the next generation of leaders while continuing to utilize the wisdom and talents of the present cohort of leadership.

The resource materials include a list of the study's seventy-seven participants with their titles and occupational affiliations, followed by a list of speeches and reports by participants made available to the researchers as part of the data. Also included are the proposal for the Wingspread Conference and the themes and questions discussed during this conference that provided the stimulus and basis for the design of our study. Finally, we provide the study's interview guide and questionnaire.

Acknowledgments

In undertaking this study, we have benefited considerably from our active involvement in the women's movement. The timing of our own scholarly work and activism places us squarely in the Instigator cohort.

This project was made possible through the financial support provided by the Ford Foundation through Alison Bernstein, by the Exxon Education Foundation through Richard Johnson, and by the Teachers Insurance and Annuity Association (TIAA) and its affiliate, College Retirement Equities Fund (CREF), through Peggy Heim. We are grateful to them for this support.

The conference at Wingspread was sponsored and supported by the Johnson Foundation. Rita Goodman deserves special thanks for her role in that meeting. As always, she knew what the important issues were and how to bring the right people together in an environment of beauty and gracious hospitality to reflect, analyze, and envision the future.

We were also assisted in many of the administrative and study details and helped by the perceptive comments and insights of our graduate students: Doris Barahona, Betty Glick, Michelle Riley, and Karen Twede. Genevieve Offner labored over the transcriptions of the interviews and the typing of numerous drafts. The Communications and Processing Center of the Graduate School of Education at the University of California, Los Angeles (UCLA), also typed and retyped the manuscript, and we thank those involved for their valuable assistance. Therese Mahoney typed the final version of the manuscript with patience and great care. We appreciate Mark Rosin's editorial assistance, as well as the help and guidance provided by Gracia Alkema, former senior editor at Jossey-Bass, and our current editor, Rebecca McGovern. We are especially grateful for the support and encouragement of Francine Deutsch and Alexander Astin, our friends, colleagues, and partners. We needed their love and wisdom throughout this process.

We dedicate this book to the memory of Joseph Katz, who brought us together many years ago through a study of adult women that he was directing at the Institute for the Study of Human Problems at Stanford University. After that initial effort, we collaborated on a number of other studies and activities on behalf of women and of education. His gifts to us enriched our lives, our friendship, and our professional commitments.

June 1991   Helen S. Astin
                                                    Los Angeles, California

                                                        Carole Leland
                                                    San Diego, California

*In memory
of our colleague and friend,
Joseph Katz*

THE AUTHORS

Helen S. Astin, a psychologist, is professor of higher education and associate director of the Higher Education Research Institute at UCLA. She received her B.A. degree (1953) from Adelphi University and her M.S. degree (1954) from Ohio University, both in psychology. She received her Ph.D. degree (1957) from the University of Maryland, also in psychology. She holds honorary doctoral degrees from Marymount Manhattan College and the American College of Switzerland.

Astin is currently a member of the board of the National Council for Research on Women, a member of the Committee on Women's Employment and Related Social Issues of the National Research Council, and a trustee of Mount St. Mary's College in Los Angeles. She has been president of the Division of the Psychology of Women of the American Psychological Association. Astin has been honored with the Award for Outstanding Contribution to Research and Literature of the National Association of Student Personnel Administrators, is a recipient of the Bread and Roses Award of the Los Angeles Westside National Women's Political Caucus, and was named a Distinguished Leader for Women in Psychology by the American Psychological Association's Committee on Women in Psychology. She has published numerous articles and ten books, including *The Woman Doctorate in America* (1969), *Some Action of Her Own: The Adult Woman and Higher Education* (1976), and *Higher Education and the Disadvantaged Student* (1972).

From 1983 to 1987, she served as associate provost of UCLA's College of Letters and Science. Before coming to UCLA, she was director of research and education for the University Research Corporation in Washington, D.C.

Carole A. Leland, a social scientist, is senior program associate for the Center for Creative Leadership at its San Diego, California, branch, where she has managed the Executive Women Workshop and the Workshop in Organizational Action. She received her B.A. degree (1956) from Syracuse University in English. She received her M.Ed. (1958) from Harvard University and her Ph.D. (1966) from Stanford University in higher education and sociology.

Leland is a frequent consultant to colleges, universities, foundations, and government agencies on problems associated with experiential learning, executive development, organization design, and education-industry cooperation. She has served as a trustee of Pratt Institute in New York and was appointed to the first Commission on Women for the American Council on Education. Currently, she is on the board of the National Society for Internships and Experiential Education and is a trustee of Northrup University.

From 1983 to 1990, Leland served as director of cooperative education and coordinator of academically related work experiences at San Diego State University. She has held faculty and administrative posts at Pennsylvania State University, the City University of New York, Columbia University, Brown University, where she was director of a research project on coeducation, "Men and Women Learning Together," and the College Entrance Examination Board.

WOMEN of INFLUENCE, WOMEN of VISION

A Cross-Generational Study
of Leaders and Social Change

CHAPTER 1

A New Perspective on Leadership

[Leadership] takes place when a certain combination of elements come together, where something needs to be done and enough people want to do it, and there's the right combination of the people that have the ideas and the people who understand the process. . . . Leadership you earn by being able to put together that right combination of things so that people are doing what they want to do.

—*Instigator*

This study is one of women leaders and of leadership through empowerment and collective action. If as feminist scholars we are correct that women have a different view of power, then a study of women leaders offers an opportunity to enhance knowledge and behavior involved in transformational leadership and specifically in empowerment.

The definition of power as empowerment treats power as an expandable resource that is produced and shared through interaction by leader and followers alike. This conception views power as energy that transforms oneself and others, and identifies the effective leader as one who empowers others to act in their own interests (Carroll, 1984). Warren Bennis and Burt Nanus (1985) also refer to power as energy, but as a social energy that is created transactionally between the leader and the led. Under these circumstances the leader perceives power as a unit of exchange, and in empowering others, empowers himself or herself. But in spite of this renewed discussion of transformational leadership and recent interest in empowerment, feminist scholars have been critical of past studies on leadership because of their male bias, reflected in their exclusion of women as the subject of study and their conception of power as domination and control (Carroll, 1984).

Gender and Leadership

In the last two decades the study of women has produced an impressive body of new knowledge and has contributed to the development of new paradigms on leadership. Feminists in search of new approaches have been able to make considerable use of the work of Thomas Kuhn, as presented in his classic volume *The Structure of Scientific Revolutions* (1970). In this work Kuhn presents a model for fundamental change in our theories and scientific paradigms. He argues that it is only by confronting "anomalies" that we have been able to challenge and reverse the traditional "paradigms" in "normal science." He points out (1970, pp. 90-91) that "confronted with anomaly or with crisis, scientists take a different attitude toward existing paradigms, and the nature of their research changes accordingly." Women's studies is the direct result of the awareness of anomalies in the traditional disciplines and in their theories.

Since the study of leadership is no exception in presenting us both with anomaly and with a crisis, the paradigms developed in women's studies offer alternative models in the study of leadership, particularly an interdisciplinary approach that may shed new light on the nature of leadership. Women's studies has been described by Florence Howe (in Boxer, 1982, p. 681) as interdisciplinary and unifying. It assumes a problem-solving stance, it is value clarifying, and it strives to promote socially useful ends. We believe that all of these parameters should be helpful in guiding our investigation of leadership.

The early research on gender and leadership was driven by two important questions: (1) Why are so few women in "positions" of leadership? (2) What are the personal and institutional roots of gender differences in access to leadership roles? These questions raise other concerns: First, how legitimate are the theories about leadership in terms of what they say about women and men? Are the theories just? And second, in terms of the larger society and its structure of opportunity, what is happening in the social system and in our institutions that prevents women from entering leadership positions in proportion to the number of talented women available?

Previous studies have focused on differences in the traits and leadership styles of women and men, and on stereotyped expectations imposed on women with respect to their leadership ability. That approach has led researchers to question whether the traditional frameworks used to study leadership can adequately explain women's behavior. For example, in a review of the empirical literature, Stephen M. Brown (1979, p. 595) concludes that "one of the popular reasons given for the differential treatment of women in management stems from stereotyping females as ineffective leaders. . . . The trait studies consistently supported the traditional attitude that women lack adequate leadership characteristics."

Studies using students have found more stereotyped beliefs about women's leadership style and effectiveness than studies with actual managers have. Brown ends his analysis with a plea that future studies should be more sensitive to the subjects used and to the methodologies applied. In other words, can studies that replicate the early models of laboratory experiments to identify differential traits, styles, and effectiveness do justice to our understanding of what leadership is all about? Or do we need to reconceptualize our definition of outcomes—that is, what we study, who we study, and under what conditions?

What feminist scholars have found is that the "anomaly," in Kuhnian terms, is multifaceted. One anomaly is that there are few women in leadership roles, in part the result of our having defined leadership solely in terms of *position*. Another anomaly is that we developed the "great *man*" theory, or the notion that "if good managers are masculine what are bad managers?" (this was the title of a recent article in the *Sex Roles: A Journal of Research;* see Powell and Butterfield, 1984). Contrary to popular belief, female leaders are not more emotional, more suggestible, less decisive, or less objective than male leaders. A further anomaly is that whereas there are no consistent gender differences among leaders, research suggests that subordinates attribute differences and react differently to similar behaviors depending on whether these behaviors are exhibited by men or women (Morrison, White, and Van Velsor, 1987).

In their book *Women and Work* (1981, p. 83) Veronica Nieva and Barbara Gutek indicate that "traditionally, women are seen as not possessing the necessary attributes for leadership. They are believed to be compliant, submissive, emotional, and to have great difficulty in making choices." Most studies that examine gender differences in personality traits of leaders do not demonstrate significant differences between women and men. Thus Nieva and Gutek suggest that reported differences reflect subordinates' perceptions. Male and female behaviors that are in line with gender-role expectations are evaluated positively. For example, "considerate female behavior is valued more than considerate male behavior, and male initiating behavior is assessed more positively than female initiation." The authors also propose (1981, p. 92) that "leader *power*, more than style or personality, may be the critical determinant of subordinate response." More recently, Florence Guido-DiBrito, D. Stanley Carpenter, and William DiBrito (1986) suggest that whereas women once were rejected for exhibiting stereotypically female behavior, such behaviors are considered to be appropriate management behavior today. However, women exhibiting participative and democratic behaviors are judged more favorably by their subordinates than are men when they exhibit such behaviors. Other recent studies indicate that employers are beginning to respond more equally to women and men who exhibit stereotypically male (structuring) as well as stereotypically female (consideration) behaviors. In terms of social change, these newer studies do offer some optimism for equality in the workplace.

It is important to note, however, that these recent studies on gender and leadership have depended on traditional theoretical models—the trait, contingency, and situational approaches—and they have often used laboratory experiments with traditional instrumentation. Even though the objective was to understand what accounts for observed differences in the participation and exercise of leadership between women and men, the paradigms have been those derived from the traditional disciplines. Despite their contributions, these studies leave us to grapple with several significant questions: Do traditional institutional structures perpetuate inequities? Does the "great man" theory suggest that leadership is finite, that only some have it, while most do not, especially women? Is the traditional notion of power as the control of resources, or the traditional concept of a leader as one who occupies a high position, a hierarchical representation of leadership that defies the notion of empowering and collective leadership? Does the paradigm of leader-follower further reinforce a hierarchical conception of leadership?

In his book *The Leadership Factor* (1988, p. 16), John Kotter offers a useful perspective on the concept of leadership: "The word 'leadership' is used in two basic ways in everyday conversation: (1) to refer to the process of moving a group (or groups) of people in some direction through (mostly) noncoercive means, and (2) to refer to people who are in roles where leadership (the first definition) is expected. In normal conversation, the second definition is most common."

We agree with Kotter's distinction, and in this study we present an examination of leaders engaged in both individual and collective action for the social "good." In addition, we believe that to expand our understanding of leadership we must ask what the goal of leadership is, study the nature of collective leadership, and redefine leadership beyond position. Thus our study's objectives are consistent with conclusions reached by Edwin Hollander (1985) in his thorough review of "Leadership and Power" in the *Handbook of Social Psychology*. He underscores the need for macro-level studies—that is, studies that look at leaders of social movements. He reminds us that we have asked questions about whether a leader has been influential and to what degree, but have not investigated the end that this behavior is directed toward. He asks us to put aside our preoccupation with the effects of leader behavior on followers and begin to understand the origins of leadership and the motivational factors in leaders, and to pose questions about leaders' self-perceptions and expectations. He suggests that we design studies that extend over time and establish links between leader motives, aspirations, and actions. In his view, the dynamic feature of leadership succession has been ignored. Finally, he urges us to undertake studies that examine contextual factors that go beyond leader activity through the exercise of influence or power and to pay more attention to the wider range and meaning of behaviors in the leader role.

Driven by a desire to expand the concept of leadership and to contribute some fresh insights to the body of literature in this field, we designed this study to provide a historical and developmental perspective on leadership. The study looks at the origins of and motives for leadership and examines leadership inheritance by describing and analyzing characteristics and behaviors of three generations of women in visible leadership roles.

Throughout this book we present our findings about women leaders and leadership by underscoring the three main foci of our study of leadership. We discuss *generational* differences because of the importance of the historical times and social context in the development of leaders and in the exercise of leadership. We compare and contrast *positional* and *nonpositional* leaders because we want to expand the conception of leadership beyond position. A great deal of our observations and commentary has focused on the *Instigators* because we conceive of leadership as a creative process that results in societal change to improve our human condition.

In designing the study we devised a conceptual framework that includes five key elements, similar to those identified subsequently by Hollander (1985). These elements are:

1. *The Positional Role of Leadership.* The study includes women leaders in visible positions within formal structures (such as presidents and directors of organizations) as well as women who have provided and are still providing leadership outside the formal structures. It includes scholars breaking new ground in contributing to social change by their published work, and women who created new forms of organizations and institutions—for example, the Feminist Press (a press designed to stimulate the publication of feminist scholarship) and Catalyst (an organization aimed at helping corporations to foster the career and leadership development of women).

2. *The Macro-Level Analysis of Leadership.* The study was designed to examine the role of leadership in social change. The

focus of the study is on women leaders who have not just made contributions to specific organizations or institutions but who have helped improve the situation of women in our society as a whole.

3. *The Origins of and Motives for Leadership.* The study was not designed to examine the leaders' effects on followers. Rather, it looks at the experiences of women leaders while they were growing up and explores the factors that prompted their interest in social change. We were interested in how leaders emerge and how they behave, and also in how the changing culture—the new or evolving social context—affects their self-perceptions and expectations.

4. *Leadership Succession.* What is the process by which new leaders emerge to continue the work that others have started? How are leaders identified, nurtured, and developed? What is the effect of role models and mentors in leadership succession? The study was designed to examine the leadership of different generations and interactions among them.

5. *The Nature of Shared Leadership.* By focusing on the networks and support systems developed and used by women leaders, and by looking at the process of empowerment, we hoped to provide insights about the nature of shared leadership.

Leadership manifests itself through activity aimed at bringing about change in an organization or institution or social system in order to improve people's lives. While to manage is to ensure that the system functions at its optimum level, leadership as a creative process results in change. In the study we conceptualized leadership as the actions and behaviors of women who worked toward changing social institutions in order to improve women's lives.

A Conceptual Framework

Our conceptual framework was rooted in a feminist perspective, and the study was designed to explore women's experience in leadership roles. Three constructs found in feminist discourse guided our own analysis.

1. *The Social Construction of Reality.* Our different beliefs reflect social constructions, and knowledge about any complex social

phenomenon, such as leadership, is strongly influenced by our social, cultural, and historical context. Accepting the premise that knowledge is socially constructed challenges the existing frameworks and calls for the formulation of new conceptual models that incorporate diverse experiences and perspectives. In our case, this meant incorporating women's experience and perspectives in formulating a conceptual model of leadership.

2. *Interdependence.* People are not isolated entities, but their life experiences are closely intertwined with those of others. Once we are aware of this interdependence, it is logical to view leadership as a process of collective effort rather than as something one person does in a vacuum.

3. *Power as Energy, not Control.* A leader does not have to exercise power over others, that is, *control.* Instead she can mobilize power and engage in leadership activities that empower others—in other words, she can exercise power *with others,* or *shared power.*

With these parameters in mind, we felt that four aspects of leadership needed to be identified and examined. These became evident as we conducted the interviews and read the transcribed materials. They were: (1) the *leader* (the person as a catalytic force or facilitator), (2) the *context* within which leadership takes place (an institution broadly defined—for example, an organization, the family, the scholarly enterprise), (3) the leadership *processes* (such as communication, empowerment, collective action), and (4) the *outcomes* (desired change in an institution or organization or change that improves the quality of life).

According to this conceptual framework, leadership is a process by which members of a group are empowered to work together synergistically toward a common goal or vision that will create change, transform institutions, and thus improve the quality of life. The leader—a catalytic force—is someone who, by virtue of her position or opportunity, empowers others toward the collective action in accomplishing the goal or vision. While in popular usage the term *leader* often denotes someone who has a position, in our study the category leader included both *positional leaders,* such as heads of organizations or institutions, and *nonpositional leaders—*

for instance, university professors and other researchers who create the knowledge central to social change.

We provide two examples of leaders and leadership to illustrate the conceptual elements in this framework. The first deals with a positional leader and leadership within an organization, and the second provides an illustration of a nonpositional leader—a scholar or producer of knowledge.

I.   Positional Leadership
    A.   Context: The organization is a college or university.
    B.   Catalyst/Facilitator: The leader is the college president.
    C.   Process:
        1.   Empowerment: Strategies and style are processes by which a leader communicates values, spells out her vision, and empowers others. Delegating responsibilities and sharing power are aspects of the empowerment process; the rewards and supports a leader provides also illustrate the process of empowerment. Thus, empowerment represents a process by which a leader provides a climate where each group member of the collective participates equally in planning and carrying out the activity.

            Carl Rogers (1978) has suggested some process elements that empower others. These include: giving autonomy to persons and groups, delegating and giving full responsibility, freeing people to do their thing, expressing one's own ideas and feelings as one aspect of the group data, offering feedback and receiving it, and finding rewards in the development and achievement of others.

        2.   Collective Action: Synergistic behavior is exhibited in the sharing of responsibilities. Tasks are distributed according to each group member's unique talents, knowledge, and expertise to enable collective action. The process by which the team develops and functions reflects the collective action. In other words, examining how the team gets formed and

works provides information and insight into the meaning of collective action.

D. Outcomes: Outcomes can be operationalized by assessing changes that improve the quality of life. Examples of such changes within an institution of higher education can include measures of students' talent development and of faculty and staff members' productivity and satisfaction with their work. In other words, in assessing outcomes we need to assess whether the members of the community (or institution) have opportunities for self-actualization and self-fulfillment.

In summary, according to this framework, any study of leadership should identify measurable outcomes, such as changes that improve the quality of life, and should assess the means and processes of leadership—for example, collective action of the members of the group or organization. The leader in this framework is perceived as a catalyst or facilitator who empowers others to use their talents and expertise to act collectively.

II. Nonpositional Leadership
    A. Context: The context is the scholarly or research enterprise.
    B. Catalyst/Facilitator: The leader is someone who has produced scholarly work that has made a difference in the lives of other people.
    C. Process:
        1. Empowerment: In this case empowerment is the process by which the scholarly work affects the personal lives of those (that is, students, other scholars, activists) who read it or use it in their social activism.
        2. Collective action: This is action that entails the sharing of ideas and the development of a network that includes scholars and/or practitioners who expand on or use the ideas presented in the scholarship provided by the nonpositioned leaders. In her article "American Female Historians in Context, 1770–1930," Kathryn Sklar describes this type of collective action, which she labels the "associative activity

among female historians." She refers to the collectivity of women historians that has grown out of the Berkshire Conference on Women's History, which was begun over fifty years ago by women historians who felt excluded from the profession. This collectivity resulted from and benefits from sharing experiences and scholarly information.

D.   Outcomes: The outcomes of scholarship include curriculum changes, changes in institutional practices, or the passage of legislation that broadens the rights of women and others. College and university projects to integrate gender perspectives in the curriculum are examples of these outcomes, as is affirmative action legislation resulting from hearings that utilize scholarly research demonstrating inequities.

This framework is proposed as a model of feminist leadership in that it views leadership as nonhierarchical and represents the leader as a catalyst or facilitator who enables others to act collectively toward the accomplishment of a common goal. As we indicated earlier, we arrived at this approach through an interactive process. While we were influenced by feminist theory, the women's voices in the study both reinforced our thinking and suggested new ways of looking at leaders and leadership. We believe that this framework offers a promising conceptual model for the study of leadership.

Research Objectives and Procedures

The study's main objective was to document the leadership provided by women in producing social change on behalf of women in the 1960s and 1970s. However, the study is also presented as a beginning empirical investigation and test of a conceptual model of feminist leadership that includes the personal characteristics of leaders and the context, processes, and outcomes of leadership.

Since we defined the *leader* as someone who played a catalytic role and who managed to empower and mobilize others toward a collective effort to improve the quality of life, we were very interested in the question of personal values and commitments. Early experiences and other aspects of our respondents' background were assessed to shed light on how values and commitments became inculcated in these leaders.

The *context* included both formal types of organizations and new types of institutions and organizations as well as scholarly activity. It also included the historical context and its effect on the lives and actions of the three generations of women.

The *processes* included the "how" of leadership—that is, how did these women go about producing social change on behalf of women? Interviews designed to inquire into the process of empowering, team building, and collaboration included questions about personal attributes and style as well as leadership strategies. To gain further understanding of collective action and the synergistic process, we asked questions about peer relationships, mentors and role models, working relationships, and networks.

The leadership *outcomes* included the programs, activities, new organizations, and research intended to change and improve the status of women in society.

The initial focus of the project was on the group of women we designated "Instigators" because their leadership shaped efforts in the 1960s and 1970s that have resulted in significant societal changes on behalf of women. However, we chose to include two other generational groups: "Predecessors" and "Inheritors." The Predecessors are women who had visible leadership roles as early as the 1950s—that is, prior to the women's movement. They included presidents of women's colleges or deans with special concerns for student affairs and women's issues, these having been the leadership roles most often available to women in that era. The Inheritors include women who are currently in leadership roles, women who have, in effect, "inherited" the issues, changes, and in some cases, the special programs and organizations formulated through the women's movement.

The historical context is an important parameter in a study of societal change. Our study was designed to examine leadership on behalf of women mainly during the span of three decades (the 1950s, 1960s, and 1970s). Including three generations of women in the sample who were visibly active during each of the three decades enabled us to study the phenomenon of succession. It also allowed consideration of developmental themes and generational issues for leaders who have experienced the total span of the time frame in question—the period of the contemporary women's movement—in contrast to a group of leaders who have only recently demonstrated visible leadership on behalf of women. The total sample of the study included seventy-seven women who span these three generations (seventeen Predecessors, thirty-one Instigators, and twenty-nine Inheritors).

The seventy-seven women were selected from four broad categories: (1) thirty-eight leaders in educational institutions, foundations, and governmental agencies; (2) fifteen leaders in national educational and professional associations and independent agencies; (3) nine heads of special programs for and about women and founders or publishers of educational publications about women; and (4) fifteen scholars and other researchers. Within each of these four categories we identified Predecessors, Instigators, and Inheritors.

While the study examines leadership and the lives of those women across three different generational cohorts, it also compares and contrasts leadership as experienced and performed by women in positional leadership roles (presidents and directors of institutions and organizations), as well as women who provided leadership through their scholarly work or writing—the nonpositional leaders.

We used a multipronged approach to identify the women we included in the sample. However, the study sample is by no means inclusive. Initially, we generated some names from our own knowledge, experience, and readings. Subsequently, the women we identified became an important source of additional names of Instigators and Predecessors. The Inheritors were generated primarily by the Instigators; they are younger women who assumed leadership around the mid 1970s within the same or similar educational settings, or they represent women who have been mentored by the Instigators themselves.

As a qualitative study, our research employed a descriptive, cross-sectional approach with separate case-study data sets for each of the seventy-seven participants. Each case study included a personal, in-depth interview of one and one-half to two hours, a background questionnaire, and supporting materials. The interviews focused on five main areas: (1) the *social and historical context* to establish the role(s) and activities of participants in the period of the mid 1950s to the late 1970s, with special reference to the issues of the women's movement; (2) the *leadership process itself* to identify antecedents, characteristics, styles and strategies, critical events, and other key elements of leadership; (3) *peer and work relationships,* including mentoring, support networks, and the role of peers and colleagues as change agents; (4) *personal and professional development,* especially the demands and satisfactions of leadership, sources of personal support and replenishment, and career and personal agendas for the future; and (5) *issues and legacies of the women's movement,* including assessment of accomplishments, current and future issues, and the inheritance of leadership responsibilities. In addition to the interviews, the background questionnaires provided information on demographic characteristics, personal and professional activities, and self-assessment (with respect to leadership attributes, life events and personal issues, and future directions). The additional supporting materials included relevant publications and biographical documentation—books, articles, speeches, interviews, and so on—that detailed individual interests and accomplishments as well as educational and societal commitments. (See the resource for a more detailed description of the sample and categories in the interview schedule and questionnaire.)

This study and its theoretical framework represent an effort to break away from earlier conceptual models and studies of leadership by redefining who a leader is beyond her or his position; by identifying the ends or outcomes of leadership—in this case, societal changes on behalf of women; and by analyzing the processes of *empowerment* and *collective action*. In designing our study and analyzing our data, however, we have drawn on the insights and tools provided by recent feminist theory, the history of women and of social movements in general, and developmental psychology and the sociology of organizations and social systems. This indebtedness will become clear in the following chapters.

CHAPTER 2

In the Spirit of the Times: Three Generations of Women Leaders

> The spread of feminism is the most spectacular, extraordinary phenomenon in the last twenty years, and I believe we will accomplish our goals in a million different ways.
>
> —*Eleanor Holmes Norton*
> *Professor of Law*
> *Georgetown University*

Eleanor Holmes Norton made the preceding statement at a small women's conference in 1983, the Wingspread Conference, which was organized as a prelude to our study on leadership. The conference's agenda was to assess the issues and leadership demands spanning twenty-five years of the modern women's movement, and to project a feminist agenda for the 1990s. Norton's comment captures the breadth and diversity of both past and future women's issues.

It was, in fact, June 1966 when twenty-eight women joined together and formed a national action organization, the National Organization for Women (NOW), whose goal was to "bring women into full participation in the mainstream of American society now, assuming all the privileges and responsibilities thereof in a truly equal partnership with men" (Freeman, 1975, p. 55). The action

15

agenda was to combat all existing forms of gender discrimination in the social institutions of the United States and to fight for the legal and economic rights of women.

The time was right: There was a nucleus of highly educated women who had experienced personal discrimination and who had learned from the successes and the problems of the civil rights movement and other direct involvement in social and political causes. President John F. Kennedy's Commission on the Status of Women, the state commissions, Betty Friedan's *The Feminine Mystique* (1963), and several visible, articulate, committed feminist legislators, including Martha Griffiths, Edith Green, Shirley Chisholm, Patsy Mink, and Ella Grasso, set the pace for the 1960s. Once the movement got underway, it quickly gained momentum. Groups that sprang up all over the country reached out and attracted different kinds of women with a wide variety of feminist commitments.

In the 1983 Wingspread session, another participant, Catharine R. Stimpson, professor of English and director at that time of the Institute for Research on Women at Rutgers University, reflected on the influence that the women's movement had had at that point. In part, she said: "In terms of public consciousness, we have made women an issue, and this has spilled over into the media, the arts, and culture. In terms of the family, we have made women, in their role as the only domestic worker, problematic; we have made violence and abuse an issue; we have suggested ways of combining work and family life; we have made reproductive choice of importance, both personally and politically. In terms of the law, we have made equality—sexual equality—an operative principle."

One further commentary from the Wingspread meeting highlights the perspectives and experiences of two decades and points to the sometime painful consequences of participation in social movements. Aileen Hernandez, an early NOW leader, commented as follows on the price many pioneering feminist leaders paid:

There will be no way that any present leader of the feminist movement could have gotten where she got without a substantial amount of things that went before. To pave the way, there were the people who took all the slurs, and all the slings and arrows . . . while feminism was being made respectable in our society, because it wasn't always considered respectable. The early people out there talking about some of the issues that we're now talking about—were very much condemned, very much put up for ridicule, and if you didn't develop some sort of a sense of protective humor on your own, you wound up with all kinds of hysteria when you tried to figure out whether you were making progress at all. I think many of the people who sat down in the early days of the second wave of feminism thought of themselves as revolutionary. But if you go back and look at some of the documents that they put together, they were hardly revolutionary. They did bring a perspective that had not before been brought to some of the things that were very much a part of our society. And looking back at the original purpose statement of NOW, it's amazing how much that still stands up with relatively few exceptions as a social document.

These views capture basic aspects of the contemporary women's movement. Certainly this movement has made women and their lives a pervasive, public issue. And, not inconsequentially, it has made feminism and the feminist agenda respectable, coherent, and compelling, not only for women but for many men as well.

The study whose results are presented in this book provided opportunities to build further on the Wingspread discussions. Through the leaders—their interviews, speeches, and publications—we report the issues and concerns that drew their energies twenty-five, even thirty years ago, and that often fire their rhetoric today. We asked the study participants who instigated institutional changes on behalf of women in the 1960s and 1970s, as well as their Predecessors and Inheritors, to trace the events and outcomes of those years, to remind us of initial concerns, to highlight accomplishments, and to project priorities for a future feminist agenda. As we interviewed the Instigators we listened for experiences and observations that provoked their initiatives and the challenges they offered to traditional structures that impeded women. We attempted to discern whether those issues were the same for the prior generation, the Predecessors. With the Inheritors, we wanted to understand their perceptions of the legacy they received—the successes and failures of the women's movement to date.

In this chapter, we provide the context of the early years of the modern women's movement. In effect, we offer a backdrop against which our leaders' assessments of past and future events can be measured, in particular, their assessment of major issues that emerged and rallied early support. We include personal experiences and reflections about the stirrings of female identity and consciousness, the lack of access to education and jobs, and gaps in intellectual inquiry and scholarship because women and their contributions were omitted. This chapter draws information from interviews as well as other sources the participants made available to us. For quotations from public documents such as speeches we have provided appropriate attribution, in contrast to interview and survey responses, where we have honored our commitment to confidentiality.

Chapters that follow describe and analyze characteristics and behaviors of individual women functioning in visible leadership roles during the origins and growth of a complex, powerful social movement. In their interview comments and in their speeches, the leaders underscore an assumption with which we began the study: that the women in key roles for educational change and leadership during the last three decades did not constitute a cohesive, connected, calculated band of women determined to overturn the traditional social institutions. Frequently their leadership was exercised independently with modest expectations and limited means. Their commitment drew strength from family roots or from individual confrontations with inequity. As their initial efforts gained visibility, the contagion of shared experiences and heightened expectations facilitated feminist solidarity and commitment to the larger goals that distinguish the modern women's movement. The leaders in this study represent diverse social and educational backgrounds, personal and family relationships, values, and the more obvious generational dimensions of age and professional experience. While aspects of their styles, political ties, and even standards for assessing the outcomes of their performances tend to separate them, they are united by their passionate, consistent dedication to personal and social justice for women throughout the world. They also report their own experiences of discrimination, isolation, and personal humiliation so similarly as to make the condition of women seem painfully singular.

Often united in their goals, the women in the study did not, however, espouse the same feminist theory or philosophy, nor for that matter did they all feel comfortable with the designation "feminist." While for many leaders the feminist identity had long been a part of their existence, for others it was a matter of time and experience before a language and an identity could be formed around feminism. And for some women the connotation of feminism remains inextricably bound up with political and economic ideologies they do not totally embrace. But despite the delayed commitment to feminism for some, or the discomfort with the language or politics of feminist thought for others, the women in the study adhered to, and often championed, what others have defined as feminist: "a system of ideas and practices which assumes that men and women must share equally in the work, in the privileges, in the defining and the dreaming of the world" (Lerner, 1984, p. 33).

Early Rallying Points

If the educational leaders studied here found common purpose— despite diverse backgrounds and the absence of conscious, well-formulated strategies for change—what major social issues fueled their energies and triggered leadership initiatives? Three areas drew significant attention: (1) concerns about female identity and consciousness; (2) access and opportunity in institutions, organizations, and the workplace; and (3) the inclusion of women in intellectual inquiry, publication, and curricular reform.

Female Identity and Consciousness. Some of the earliest efforts on behalf of women preceded the founding of NOW and the publication of Friedan's *The Feminine Mystique.* In the late 1950s, for example, the Radcliffe Institute for Independent Study, though garbed in a quite traditional and distinctive academic identity, symbolized some of the early stirrings of the women's movement. On a number of occasions, Mary I. Bunting, then president of Radcliffe, spoke of the roots of the now-famous institute and often called attention to the special needs and problems of women. In one speech titled "The University's Responsibility in Educating Women for Leadership," presented at Southern Methodist University in January 1966, she helped to elaborate the issues she and her Radcliffe colleagues addressed in making what at that time (1959) seemed revolutionary in the scheme of American higher education: "It was a few statistics that sparked my interest in the special problems faced by women. . . . The statistic that jarred me was the finding during the post-Sputnik period of national soul-searching that of those high school students who scored in the top 10 percent by ability tests and did not go on to college, more than 95 percent were girls. It wasn't so much the waste of a national resource that bothered me as the satisfactions that I believed these girls were missing in life. How had they happened to decide against college?" She had explored this problem in a convocation address, "Education and Evolution," at Vassar College a few years earlier, in October 1961. "I am constantly discouraged by the forces that tend to shunt girls into terminal programs at all levels of education. Nowhere is this crippling guidance more evident than in the handling of girls who have the potentialities for making important contributions in the sciences and getting great personal satisfaction from such endeavor. They are discouraged from taking physics in high school, urged not to take College Boards in chemistry even if they elected the subject, and in college warned not to plunge in as freshmen. The climate of unexpectation as to what women may do with their education has led to all the hidden dissuaders in our culture that tend to ridicule our vaunted freedom of opportunity. . . . If any group of students needs basic education it is women, who will later face interruptions and geographic dislocations that will call for the greatest flexibility." The Radcliffe Institute was founded to remedy precisely this kind of problem. In her address at an invitational conference at Radcliffe College in April 1972 ("Women: Resource for a Changing World"), Bunting stated:

The Radcliffe Institute was conceived as a laboratory with a mission and also as a center of continuing education. We wanted a laboratory in order to find better ways of helping women do the things they wished to do and we wanted a center of continuing education to maintain programs that the laboratory found promising.

It was my belief in 1960 that the central problem in women's education stemmed from confusion about its goals. Although largely unrecognized then, it was generally assumed that women could not be expected to contribute significantly to intellectual advances in any rigorous field of study or action. One educated women for the greater pleasure and support they could provide as wives and mothers, as school teachers and research associates, but not for what they might accomplish intellectually in their own right. The further they advanced in their studies, the less support they received. Families and institutions that cared strenuously about whether a bright applicant was admitted as a freshman took little interest in whether she completed her doctorate or got a good medical residency. No wonder women undergraduates were confused. . . . If, however, Radcliffe College were to demonstrate its concern by aiding those women who wished to pursue advanced studies or research, might that not make an impression? . . . A laboratory seemed the logical answer. Hopefully, its very establishment would convey our concern and whatever we learned would be instructive to others.

In the late 1950s and early 1960s, other programs for women, frequently sponsored through adult education centers or university extension divisions, responded to the needs of women for personal assessment of skills and experiences and for help with educational and occupational choices. Program leadership often came from women who either had the same needs and spearheaded proposals to promote formal programs, or from women whose scholarly research and astute observations shifted their attention from volunteer social service or other endeavors to initiatives on behalf of other women: "The reason I became interested in programs for women was that I began to notice that women, who otherwise were very bright and very well-educated, weren't participating in discussions. They were sitting very quietly and the men were having a great time with topics like 'Who's responsible for clean water in the environment?' The women would sit in these groups very quietly, obviously listening, but almost never asking a question. Certainly almost never offering an opinion on these subjects." This leader's assessment of the situation prompted her to develop a special television series for women in 1964: "We organized some 200 viewing groups that met in people's living rooms, in churches and temples, in factories, in church basements, anywhere that people could gather. We put out discussion materials, trained discussion leaders, and altogether had about 3,000 persons, primarily women, watching the programs."

Some years later another study participant, M. Elizabeth Tidball, professor of physiology at the George Washington University Medical Center, captured the essence of the continued rarity of women in the male world and the painful identity crisis women faced as a result. In a speech at the inauguration of the president of Russell Sage College in October 1976 ("Toward Developing a Common Perspective"), she said:

> Virtually all work roles that men occupy are defined in masculine terms to such an extent that the attributes associated with the job description are indistinguishable from the attributes associated with masculinity. Analytic thought is "male" thought; the natural sciences are the "hard" sciences; the procedure of research in any field is to "attack" problems; the goal teachers hold for their students is to "master" a discipline. Valued behavior is "potent." Valued creations are "seminal."
>
> In this paradigm, where sex role and occupational role share a common identity, where being and doing coalesce, what does higher education and what does society offer to women? From children's books, the mass media, popular magazines, and behavior in the classroom, girls and boys, women and men, learn that the accepted roles for females are: wife, mother, witch, good fairy, beautiful queen, and sex kitten. . . . If a woman is exceptionally bright and reasonably unfeminine, she may aspire to become one of the boys, but with the caveat that in so doing she can be classified only as a low-status male and will likely remain low man on the totem

pole. Why, one must wonder, was anyone surprised to learn of the fear of success among bright young women?

An awareness of the political dimension of their personal situations began to grow in academic women. In her interview, one faculty woman talked about her heightened sensitivities this way: "When I began to read women's novels and women's literature, the sort of Betty Friedan–style analysis, it hit home. . . . I was particularly full of resentment at having to leave my own graduate work in the middle and relocate, leave my family, leave school. . . . I was raging with anger and upset at having to move and also I felt [my husband] was not as smart as I was in some ways, but I was having to relocate to follow him."

Although academic women used their professional roles to initiate and orchestrate the early activities for women, nonetheless they frequently remained isolated, sometimes being "tokens" in predominantly male departments and institutions. They, like the women they served, sought some form of connectedness in consciousness-raising groups: "I remember going to one of my best friends and saying, 'Let's get together a group and start talking about things.' Of course, women were doing this all over the country but we didn't know that. It was so organic. I remember the first night we met, there were about eight of us. The next time we met a week later there were about forty women who came. We had to divide up and we numbered off into ones into one group, twos in another group, and so on. . . . My group met for four years." Such experiences, duplicated across the nation, gave strength and momentum to the quest for a female identity.

Access and Opportunity. Issues of personal identity and consciousness merged with problems of access and opportunity. Access issues revolved around the availability of part-time education, flexible class schedules, and financial aid, especially for married women. Women encountered these barriers as they awakened to what a few early leaders had imparted—the idea that women were entitled to develop their own talents and to share educational and job opportunities equally with men. Sometimes women ran smack into humiliating injustices: "I had difficulty after passing my Ph.D. orals in getting a fellowship for my last year, for my dissertation. I talked with the department. . . . 'Aren't you going to go where your husband goes? You'll probably get pregnant. Why should we invest in you?' And I said, because I've been here three years. I've gotten through my exams. I've got a dissertation topic. I've got data because I've been part of this national research team. . . . But here I was at twenty-five, for the first time fighting a system that was saying, 'We don't think you're going to do anything for the discipline.' And so within about a fifteen-month period, my head started turning."

Women responded by pushing for platforms to air issues as well as by establishing connections with other women. In some instances, women graduate students demanded greater visibility for women in professional organizations. In other cases, professional women connected through established committees or task forces. Often the professional associations offered acknowledgment and forums on major issues of access and equity. Tidball, in her speech at Russell Sage College, described this progress as follows:

During the past few years there has been a most striking development, the emergence of a new phenomenon, that can be characterized as the working together of women in groups for assistance, support, and affirmation of their non-biological creativity. Committees and task forces within virtually all the professions, large federated groups, scholarly journals, and conferences of all sizes and agendas have served to bring professional women together. For academic women there is at last a means to come out of the isolation of the campus, to meet others, to exchange ideas and concerns both professional and personal, to begin to know for the first time what it means to be a part of a collegial network. It is now possible for competent women to sit on committees, lead policy discussions, and direct organizations so that a linkage between accomplishment and reward is finally and rationally established. Through group activities with other women, women's self-image and self-confidence have been strengthened. . . . Women are learning new ways to acknowledge, affirm, and project both their gender identity and their professional competence as mutually compatible and interrelated facets of their beings.

While women had begun to get access to positions, they still were excluded from the male networks and informal power structures. By the early 1970s, women leaders recognized the inequities and voiced their concerns publicly to herald changes that would affect generations to come. Nancy Schlossberg, in "Rumblings of a Mad Feminist," a paper presented at a meeting of the American Council on Education in May 1974, said the following:

As I think about the future I begin to see a mission for myself. Others are working to help women become more assertive, ready for success, and for the first big job. Men and women are beginning to push selection committees to go that next step beyond just accumulating women's vitae and papers but to actually select women. My mission is to help those who get selected so that they won't fall into the trap that I did. Since women don't room with the Clark Kerrs, the Robert Hutchins; since women do not eat at many of the clubs with the power elite; since women are not part of the establishment which includes the informal as well as the formal socialization process, those of us who know what it feels like to be on the inside can help sensitize women to what is in store so that they don't fall into the naive trap I did. It is not budgeting and discussion leading women need; it is to understand the ways of the world to which men have access and from which women are excluded.

Intellectual Inquiry and Scholarship. The initial phases of educational reform on behalf of women revolved around the world of scholarship and intellectual discourse. Instigator Catharine R. Stimpson, founding editor of *Signs: Journal of Women in Culture and Society,* pursued the significance of scholarship with Gerda Lerner, a historian who was then president of the Organization of American Historians. Stimpson asked, "Do you think feminist scholars have come closer to a correct analysis of women's situations?" To which Lerner replied: "Yes. The progress we have made is due to the collective nature of the enterprise and to the fact that we have found a way to break out of the isolation that our training imposes on us. This is exciting and new, just as the forms that the Women's Movement has found for solving social problems have been innovative. For instance, the women's group, the support group, women's health services, interage housing, and other living schemes. . . . After we realized that women's experience of the world, the female experience, is different from men's, we had to ask different questions in order to elicit this experience. All our thinking had been androcentric. In order to get to the true meaning of what we're doing, we had to find a way of removing ourselves from that" (Stimpson, 1981, p. 93).

Women scholars took on the task of grappling with enormous complexities and gaps with respect to gender differences and the inclusion of women in the knowledge base of the academic disciplines. The field of women's studies provided a major force for disseminating the "new scholarship" and for generating new research. It was also through women's studies that the conscious examination of gender-related issues began to expand, and to include far more women than the middle-class, educated suburban housewives who first challenged the barriers to identity and equity. Florence Howe (1973, p. 53), Instigator and editor of the Feminist Press, recounted her own experience of teaching an introductory women's studies course in which the students offered quite diverse perspectives: "In addition to its interracial composition, half the people in my class are lower or working class. A few are upper or upper-middle class, the age range being 17 to 60 years, and some students have as many as eight children. How do we deal with the issues of racism, sexism, and classism? We manage it by becoming a bit more sophisticated all the time, and a bit more knowledgeable about the issues. Also, we need to go beyond analysis to understanding. Until you have a history, you have no future. Until we understand where sexism and racism, our problems and illnesses, come from, we will not know how to solve them. It's much more than knowing that they exist. It's knowing where they came from and of what use they are to this nation."

What emerges from these brief comments on the subject of

identity, access, opportunity, and inclusion is, in fact, a collective agenda, focused on shared priorities for equal opportunity, professional visibility and status, and scholarly recognition and achievement. Our study also allows us to see that differences of degree and kind within the common agenda mirror the social and historical climates in which our three cohorts developed. The seventy-seven women leaders we interviewed speak in the voices of their particular generations.

Three Generations Committed to Social Change

The following comments offer a starting point for our discussion of the different perspectives of the three age cohorts we studied: "I've had a strong interest in women's right to intellectual development and women's right to the things that were of interest to them . . . and a growing awareness of the problem that women students had to deal with in a college that emphasized intellectual development but really saw the future of women as being well educated so that they could bring up families and be good wives to successful husbands" (a Predecessor). "[I found] myself handed down to the personnel assistant officer to be given a typing test . . . [and recognized] not only that it was a personal problem, that it was the fault of my personal decision to follow a man, but that there was something bigger at work" (an Instigator). "The inheritance probably begins in a conscious way, with going to a women's college, . . . to the degree to which that represents a tradition that I got both in terms of its support for young women to go on and make something of themselves and [to have as role models] the kinds of women who preceded me" (an Inheritor).

As we indicated earlier, our study began with a sample of Instigators—women who had assumed visible leadership roles during the 1960s and early 1970s, the years of the onset and growth of the modern women's movement. Very shortly, as we were proceeding with the interviews of the Instigator group, we recognized two things. First, we saw that there was another group of women, an earlier leadership cohort, that had been doing extraordinary work on behalf of women before the public pronouncements of the late 1960s. They were the Predecessors—women leaders in education and foundations whose energies and efforts were devoted to the education and career development of women. They were often deans of women, directors of the continuing education programs for women, presidents of women's colleges, and officers in foundations. Second, we identified an emerging cohort of women leaders who were gaining visibility in the organizational and institutional settings that were created or transformed by the Instigators. They were the Inheritors—women in their late thirties and early forties who had begun to provide leadership for women in the mid or late 1970s. Predecessors, Instigators, and Inheritors—three generations that were labeled as such partially by virtue of age and partially because of their experiences as leaders at particular periods of social history. As varied as their perspectives and positions might be, all share the designation of "educators."

Our study's focus on the educational sector rather than business, industry, or the political arena also reflects the social and cultural past. Historically it has been easier for women to assume leadership within education than within other institutional or organizational settings. Since the beginning of the twentieth century, demand for teachers has always turned to a women's labor pool; as a result, women have had greater access and more opportunities for visible leadership roles within the American educational system. While the outcomes this study celebrates underscore new, broader career and social opportunities for women, they also remind us of the professional barriers women still face.

As a consequence of their respective historical contexts the three generational cohorts differ in terms of personal development, educational experiences, and opportunities for work. The nature of their personal experiences, their perceptions of opportunities, and their parents' expectations and support, as well as the emergence of their own passion for and commitment to issues of justice and to improving women's lives, correspond with the climate and culture of the period in which they were born and grew up. While there are common threads across the generations, as the earlier quotations amply demonstrate, there are also disparities of perception and beliefs about women's experiences and the role and importance of education in women's lives. In the generational glimpses that fol-

low, we also see the social and cultural complexities that often
dictate approaches to leadership.

While the Predecessors grew up during the post–World War
I and pre-Depression years, the Instigators' important developmental years were during the Depression and World War II. For the
Inheritors, the important developmental years were the years of the
civil rights and anti-Vietnam protests. Each cohort has experienced
critically peculiar national times and events that have affected their
expectations, beliefs, and passions. We do not pretend to undertake
a thorough analysis of how history affects personality. This is not
our task here. We simply want to alert the reader to how historical
times appear to have shaped the choices and actions of our women
leaders.

With respect to age, over 80 percent of the Predecessors are
seventy-one years of age or older. They represent a cohort in retirement. But while two-thirds of them have retired from their formal
positions, they continue to remain professionally active by serving
on boards and commissions, by writing, and by doing volunteer
work.

The Instigators, most of whom are between the ages of fifty-
five and sixty-five, are very much involved in their careers in active
and visible roles within their college and universities or in other
social and educational organizations. The majority of Inheritors are
now in their early and mid forties. However, among the Inheritor
group we find women, similar in age to the Instigators, who found
themselves in positions of leadership at a later time because they
delayed their educational preparation, often by making choices to
marry early, raise a family, and then resume their education and
careers. Delayed professional leadership appears to be a pattern
more typical among earlier generations of women than among
women today.

Regarding early schooling, the Predecessors were much more
likely to have attended private high schools than were either of the
other two cohorts. This, too, reflects historical precedents. In earlier
years, parents who were interested in seeing that their daughters had
opportunities for higher education were more likely to invest in
private secondary education. This was not the case for the other two
cohorts. For the Instigators, and more so for the Inheritors, the

historical info.

expanding opportunities in higher education rarely necessitated investment in private high school education.

Differences were also observed with respect to educational attainment. Compared to the Instigators or Inheritors, fewer of the Predecessors hold the Ph.D. degree. Earlier generations of educators had greater access to postsecondary employment and opportunities for advancement without a Ph.D. than has been the case in more recent years, when the Ph.D. or Ed.D. appears to be essential.

With respect to marital status, not surprisingly, a higher proportion of Predecessors remained single than either of the two other groups. About one half of the Predecessors were never married compared to one in ten among the Instigators and one in ten among the Inheritors. For the earlier generations of women, it was much harder to manage a demanding career as well as marriage and a family.

In addition to conducting personal interviews, we collected information by means of a survey questionnaire on which we asked the respondents to rate themselves on a set of personal characteristics. These self-perceptions distinguish the three cohorts in ways that again suggest social mores. While all three groups revealed a considerable degree of self-confidence, the Predecessors tended to rate themselves higher on adaptability, and the Instigators assigned themselves higher ratings on autonomy, perseverance, self-discipline, and assertiveness. The Inheritors, on the other hand, tended to score themselves higher on ambition, interpersonal skills, leadership, perceptiveness, and sociability.

Of the three groups, the Predecessors generally gave themselves more average ratings overall on many of the personal traits included in the scale, compared to the Instigators or Inheritors, who tended to rate themselves above average on these traits. The difference between the Inheritor and Instigator groups appears to fall along the dimension of sociability versus autonomy, with the Instigators being much more independent and autonomous while the Inheritors are much more sociable and interpersonally oriented.

In the brief general sketches that follow we call attention to some general emphases and characteristics of each generational group designated in this study. Individual examples and further insights to elaborate similarities and distinctions among the three cohorts, however, will appear throughout the book.

Predecessors. The Predecessors focus their energy on education. They value education and they see its importance in achieving equality for women and improving women's lives. There are good reasons for this. First, most of them represent an educational elite. Not many women of their age have achieved the levels of education and professional stature that they have achieved. As one of the women put it very aptly, "[In] the cohort I came from, fewer than 5 percent went beyond high school." They were high achievers in school: "I did very well in math at college; very well." And the Predecessors received a great deal of support from their parents, especially their fathers, about achieving, doing well, becoming whatever they aspired to: "He gave me—they both did—a lot of support in what I was doing, and it was important for me to do what I wanted to do and not to worry about whether I was like other people."

Their own personal experiences and their occupational roles as leaders in colleges and universities—primarily as dean of women or president of a women's college—provided them with opportunities to articulate their concerns about education and career options for women students. What drove them was their strong interest in enabling women to achieve: "I can remember a speech I made at Sarah Lawrence, defending women's education . . . feeling defensive about women's colleges that were being talked down by various people . . . defending to parents, skeptical parents, the money they were spending on their daughter at places like Sarah Lawrence and later at Wellesley." Early women leaders concentrated on what a college education should be for women students: "I became really interested in the question: What should the college be saying to its women students? What should it expect of its women students? How do we give them encouragement to pay attention to their minds and their intellectual development?"

The Predecessors' own early leadership experiences in high school and college varied. Some of them remained uninvolved, while others participated actively and persistently. One less involved Predecessor described her experience as follows: "I was active in theater while in college . . . not involved in clubs. . . . I was an intellectual snob." While she may not have had active leadership roles, her theater work provided her with opportunities to develop her public speaking and debate skills. She described her experiences during a summer theater program at a Midwestern university as follows: "It was very good for me because part of the work was debate, and I had never heard of debate and public speaking."

Another Predecessor described her early experiences in high school in terms of scholastic achievement: "I was always the first in class." She also talked about her experiences with oration: "What it did was get me out in front of a large group and teach me that I could be in control of that situation." While she said that she was seldom elected to leadership roles in high school, she held many elected offices in college. Indeed, early leadership experiences taught these women a lot, but what they value most is the learning and self-confidence they derived from experiences on debate teams and in other public speaking activities.

The early cohort of women placed in positions of leadership were the "solo" women in their organizations. They had no role models other than the powerful men. Very often they had to adopt the male model of leadership. They also had to excel; they had to become even more exceptional than the men among their peers so that they would be listened to.

In answer to questions about leadership styles and strategies, the Predecessors consistently reported that being the only woman in a group had an important impact on their leadership style or their choice of strategy in accomplishing their goals. One woman pointed out that "the boards of the foundations I worked for were almost invariably all men." At another point, the same woman said of her experiences on a university committee that "everybody except me on that committee was of a stature, and they were all men." She chose to preface her response to our question about leadership style and strategies by first describing the context, in which "all other participants were men of great stature," and then she proceeded to say that "I did not let women down, but I used different strategies . . . and I used just plain hard reason." While she would not completely accept the label of leader—"it's a word that I'm never comfortable with"—she did attribute to herself the ability to influence the direction of the two organizations she served as an officer: "I know that both did some things they wouldn't have done if I hadn't been there, and I suppose that's leadership." But it is empowerment that she saw as the real role of leadership: "To see that I can em-power somebody to start a program and do something really big and important . . . that's wonderful." Most of all, she attributed her accomplishments to hard work: "Don't forget, it was Johann Sebastian Bach who, when asked what's the secret of your success, said, 'Work, work, work, and more work.' . . . I thrive on that."

Thus, in part, a collective profile of the Predecessor reflects someone whose life has been driven toward educational and professional achievement and one who believes in hard work and a high standard of excellence. The Predecessors' commitment to women and leadership on their behalf has centered on their belief that educational opportunities should be available to women, that the educational system should not discriminate against women, and that parents and educators should see that women have the right to an education equal to that of men. Their intellect and industry set them apart and their acceptance and visibility in influential male circles have provided them with opportunities for leadership, often leadership that could support and enhance the talents of other women. The Predecessors do not speak of experiences of discrimination but rather of being the only woman among men. Of necessity, they have worked closely with men, and men have supported them. While they are committed to equity and to women's development, they usually do not choose to describe themselves as feminists. The Predecessors are now in retirement, but they continue to remain active, primarily through their participation on boards and through other efforts to support education and their communities.

Instigators. The Instigators are the group of women we have identified as the initiators of a social movement (from the mid 1960s to the mid 1970s). They represent a cohort of visible spokespersons at the onset and during the early years of the second wave of the women's movement. They provided leadership through existing institutions or created new organizations, and their research and writing on women have had, and continue to have, an impact on challenging the patriarchal structure of existing institutions. While in later chapters we describe the lives and leadership of the Instigators in much greater detail, here we want to draw attention, once again, to the contextual influences the study emphasizes.

Three unique elements stand out in the Instigators' personal lives and in their leadership:

1.   Early experiences of personal discrimination and an acute awareness of social injustices
2.   Personal involvement on various commissions, committees, and task forces organized to examine the status of women in American society and to identify mechanisms to ameliorate discrimination
3.   Strong connections with like-minded women and recognition of the importance of networks

The Instigators encountered personal discrimination early in their lives. Whether they had the experience of being Jewish in an elite Northeastern environment, being physically handicapped, being trapped in Nazi Germany, or being poor, their personal sense of discrimination sensitized them to injustices inflicted on other oppressed groups—especially people of color and the poor. As one woman put it: "I had a strong identification with blacks, Jews, people from other cultures. I always felt a passionate zeal for justice."

Involvement with groups concerned with the status of women, whether through their research or activism, had a very strong galvanizing effect on the Instigators' feminism. This involvement also connected them with other like-minded women and a network was formed. The network provided support for their concerns; more important, it taught them the effectiveness of collective action to bring about change. They came to recognize leadership as a group effort. They are the women who see themselves as challengers of men and empowerers of women. A sense of outrage about gender discrimination in education and work, passionate feelings about issues of justice, and experience in the civil rights movement have been critical ingredients of their leadership for social change.

Being part of the civil rights movement taught them some important lessons. Many saw firsthand that Southern women involved in the civil rights movement were ostracized, and this had a profound effect: "It was the first time I thought of women as a political/social category." They were moved not only by their observations but also by further personal discrimination; as one woman said, "I had suffered the discrimination and the sense of impotence in the antiwar movement that a lot of other women felt." That led them to further inquiry and a passion for justice: "I started to read and connect with other women." NOW as a woman's political/activist organization was critical to them. Women were able to connect and to hear other women's voices. Conferences on women became an important vehicle in establishing the networks: "[A conference] glued our commitment to one another, and we were inventing the style of doing business that would be appropriate to feminist politics and to women's studies."

Leadership as practiced by the Instigators had to be collective. They empowered each other by sharing information and, some twenty years later, they believe that the women's movement spread because of this exchange—listening and letting others talk: "I want to be remembered as an empowerer."

The Instigators were the new professionals during a time of unrest, a time when women began to question unjust practices—racism, sexism, U.S. involvement in a criminal war. Personal politics infused their professional work: "I wanted to make a difference . . . and make my personal politics and professional life work together. . . . I also believe that in some way my life had to make a difference, had to count for something because I had to in some way justify my survival [from early poverty, fatal disease, Nazi Germany]."

Thus, in the words of one respondent: "Leadership is how to get something done. . . . It is partly working through other people. . . . It is partly speaking on behalf of other people . . . and [keeping] right on believing in the goodness of people." In spite of their personal pain, their belief in the goodness of other people inspired and motivated them to provide leadership for change.

As empowerers, the Instigators trust their own power; they do not feel the need to have power over others and are willing to foster and facilitate the latent strengths in the other person. Their approach is a person-centered one, the essence of empowerment in that it never takes power away from the person (Rogers, 1978). They are distinguished from the Predecessors by the urgency of their awareness and perceptiveness about injustice and inequalities and by their commitment to connect with other women in the struggle for social change.

Inheritors. Reading through the transcripts of the Inheritors' interviews, one recognizes the significant role the Instigators have played in shaping the Inheritors' feminist vision, their values, and their work. The Instigators often functioned as the Inheritors' mentors and role models: "Working under [name of person] as the woman head of an organization offered an alternative vision of what women could be as leaders." "I've learned a great deal from the generation of women before me. . . . I have never seen so many wonderful people. . . . [It was] absolutely inspirational to me to see their confidence and their ability. They seemed very much the role models to emulate."

Their mentors not only inspired them, they guided them as well: "I had a failed love affair with an undergraduate beau. . . . I saw it as a limitation of a person with relationships rather than as a systemic problem. . . . My dean of women gave me *The Feminine Mystique* as a gift when I graduated." Her dean's influence was a strong one; she assumed special importance in her life. By giving her *The Feminine Mystique* she was educating her about women's dilemma in combining work and family and about the importance of being involved outside the home so that she would not suffer from "the disease that has no name" (Friedan, 1963). The dean mentored her and also inspired her. Thus she was a very important role model for her: "When I left college I thought I wanted to be a dean of women because of her. . . . She was my only adult role model."

As these comments suggest, women served the Inheritors as role models, teachers, and friends. Invariably, Inheritors talked about the importance of women's friendship: "[Attending a women's college was] . . . a very important point in my life because I made such good friends among women and had such a good time with my women friends."

They spoke of working with other women as having been a very special experience for them: "Working with Elizabeth was sort of an unbelievable situation in which we thought in the same way, we read things in a similar way. . . . I don't think I could have worked with any man the way I worked with Elizabeth, partly because we shared a feminist commitment."

Having other feminists around has provided a great deal of support: "There is a bunch of us . . . all interested in feminist issues [who] meet once a week to [serve as] a support group and then to make weekly schedules." "I have always felt part of a wonderfully supportive group, both work group and friendship. My friendships are wonderful. If something goes wrong in my life, I have ten people on the phone calling to find out. . . . I've always had wonderful friends and a lot of times they are the same people I work with and that's always been true with me. So I would say, in fact, one of the things we've learned in this movement is how to be friends to each other. . . . If there is any benefit, it's the female friendship network, the depth of them, the resonance of them."

These friendships with other women who cared about the same issues, and who were committed to sustaining the changes accomplished by the Instigators, mean that the Inheritors depended on each other: "[We were] trying to sort of organize a group of people together to get the task done. It was pretty much in terms of "well, see, what all do we need to do in order to get this done and who is best able to do it?" The collective effort, like that of the Instigators, taught them important lessons—most especially the power of the group: "We've built our power base largely by sharing it, not by hanging onto it."

Thus, when asked about their leadership style or strategies, Inheritors talked about them in terms of the collective enterprise: "I would characterize myself as somebody who tries to find strengths that everybody has and build a team that's compatible, and to care about individuals as much as the project, and to care about how we do it as well as what we do." "What I try to do is empower the people to do things and to help other people gain self-confidence to do things on their own."

They like to see things happen. Thus, they described themselves as problem solvers: "I am a facilitator. That's what I do best, and that's what I like best. I like to make things happen, not just for the sake of their happening, but because I think they have an impact on people." "I don't start out to seek a leadership position, I start out to make something happen. I really like to be in the middle of solving problems . . . and I see myself as able to solve problems, to command resources . . . [to] look at issues and not getting stuck. . . . I do not feel timid about stating my ideas out loud, even if they get attacked." The Inheritors are doers and their positional role appears to be insignificant to them: "I have far less of a sense of myself as a public figure. I think I'm far less self-conscious about being a leader. . . . I can do what seems to be politically right and to open my mouth because I am used to opening my mouth, but not to think of myself as constructing a role of influence and preeminence."

Most of the Inheritors were in graduate school when the Instigators were actively attacking the system, creating new organizations and shaping our institutions. What is astonishing to us is the acknowledgment of their early passivity regarding issues and action: "The civil rights movement was well underway and people were going to march on Selma, but I wasn't at that time. I was busy studying and trying to do this school work." "I did not have an ideology. It was not articulated for me. . . . I wasn't part of any women's group or anything like that. . . . I had not been active in women's groups." "I had large arguments with people and said 'I never experienced any discrimination.'"

Their experience with the feminist issues and activism has, indeed, been an evolving one: "I think that the political climate of the seventies articulated for me something I had lived for a long time but never conceptualized in those terms." Unlike the Instigators, who were very conscious and articulate about such experiences, the Inheritors often deny experiencing personal discrimination. Their feminism was sparked by having had the opportunity and experience of teaching in the emerging field of women's studies and of serving in organizations, committees, and groups concerned with women's issues. For them, the social context had already begun to shift.

Many of them became politicized as they began to teach women's studies: "I think it was the first year I taught the initial Women in Literature class [in 1970]. I also was beginning to feel this wonderful exhilarating connection between what I was reading, what I was teaching, and what I was devoting myself to politically, because I began to become involved."

We sense that not having experienced overt discrimination, yet having had strong role models and having done some feminist work early in their adulthood, the Inheritors have a very different perspective from the earlier cohorts—about themselves, their relationships with women and men, and their views about the accomplishments and future of the women's movement. While they described their early involvement in women's activities rather passively, they talked about their lives and work in a most animated way: "I love teaching. . . . I like to do something I consider to be socially useful." "It was tremendously energizing to move into women's studies, I mean intellectually just the most exciting place to do work."

They are very optimistic about the future and they feel energized, in part because of the strong support they have received from their women mentors, the friendships with women peers, and the collegial relationships with contemporary men as partners and co-workers: "My husband is a very good friend to me. . . . He is just phenomenal. He is committed to the same sorts of issues. He's really an exceptional person." They are enthusiastic: "Maybe I'm always doing different things because I am constantly discovering the options. . . . They weren't all there from the beginning." "I feel sort of young and exuberant and full of possibilities." "I am not even vaguely tired or burned out. . . . I don't feel tired. I feel energized at the moment."

While they believe in the collective, in empowerment and in being enablers and facilitators, they also describe themselves as politically savvy: "I really use power in a fairly sophisticated way. . . . I've had to learn to operate in fairly tough, large-scale situations and simultaneously keep my commitment in the feminist movement." "I see myself as very much part of the establishment. . . . The power structure in New York see me as one of them, though they know full well that I have a special commitment to women." They talk of *presence* as an important element in leadership—"a presence that can be put on as one puts on a jacket."

One of the Inheritors, a college president, characterized her style as entrepreneurial: "I am more of a social entrepreneur than a financial entrepreneur." "Everyone in town will return my phone calls: the mayor, the governor, the bankers. I don't bother them very often but when I do they'll return my calls."

They are bold in their statements and the choice of words to describe themselves and others like them: "I can and do what seems to be *politically right*." "Not only do I have power, I have access to power. I can get anyone on the phone. I use my power gingerly. I pick and choose." They are politically savvy without being confrontational: "I used humor a lot. . . . I would not be confrontational and I'd usually get my way. As my mother used to say, 'You get more flies with honey than you do with vinegar.'" They attribute their style to their having been of a different generation than the earlier cohorts of women: "We were this way because I think we're more secure professionally. I think there have been more opportunities. I think we're more sophisticated politically. I think we have some understanding of power."

Unlike the Predecessors, who believe in the power of education as the vehicle for social change, and the Instigators, who have experienced the power of politics and legislative agendas in changing institutions, the Inheritors were mentored to become the sustainers of the women's movement and the feminist cause. They became aware of discrimination only after they took active roles in the movement. In the role of sustainer, they began to see the importance of increasing support among women and of embracing not only more women, but women from every class, ethnic, and racial background. To sustain a movement you need to constantly involve new people. The Inheritors are the ones who, in inheriting this important legacy, are also worrying about the "graying of the women's movement": "The way to keep this sort of second wave of feminism alive is going to require a lot more vigilance and a lot more maintenance."

Our women leaders are the progeny of their historical and social periods. They share common commitments and certainly reflect similar leadership capacities, but their experiences, styles, and aspirations pick up the themes and preoccupations of the different moments in history we have surveyed. The distinctions among generations will surface again as we look more closely at leadership by and for women.

CHAPTER 3

Becoming Leaders: Key Influences and Experiences

My grandfather has turned out to be incredibly important. If there are androgynous people, grandpa was
one of them . . . who could cry and cried if something
moved him. He clearly was boss man at the railroad.

—Inheritor

What has given these women the strength to overcome
discrimination, harassment, and rejection and to lead a movement?
Where does the assurance and belief in self derive from? Where does
this caring and passion for causes come from? To answer these
questions, we first looked at their family of origin, their relationships with parents, grandparents, and siblings. Then we incorporated the impact of mentors and role models, as well as other early
experiences.

In this and in subsequent chapters our discussion draws from
information we gathered from the three generational groups—
Predecessors, Instigators, and Inheritors—with a primary emphasis
on Instigators. However, we also attend to the experiences and behaviors of the positional as well as the nonpositional leaders (scholars and researchers), since from the start we have conceived of
leadership as both positional and nonpositional.

Family Backgrounds

Eclectic as their family backgrounds appear, the Instigators emphasized how frequently their values and leadership potential stemmed from their roots. They came from varied life situations— farms, the working class, an immigrant background, academic parents, parents with family-owned businesses, and single-parent and all-female households. The majority confirm other studies that noted strong identification of daughters with fathers but also called attention to the importance of self-actualized women in their lives. For the Instigators, often these women were their mothers.

Consistent among the Instigators was the sense that parents and families modeled, encouraged or, at the very least, allowed them to develop as independent women infused with strong beliefs in social justice and the work ethic. As the following comments show, the Instigators came from families that set standards for life performance and morality: "I have a large social conscience. I really care about issues and people, and, obviously, equity is one of those fundamental values. . . . My father and mother in very different ways were always ideological champions of the underdog. . . . My mother grew up on a farm and became a secretary . . . and my father was trained as a carpenter as a kid, but was a white-collar worker. . . . He was a very smart man but he'd never been to college. He was absolutely determined that we would all go to college." "Certainly my father and mother were both deeply involved in a great many social movements and they were activists. . . . My family has always been social action oriented." "My mother's family was raised in poverty and all became enormously wealthy, powerful people. . . . They gave out a lot of money. I don't know what effect that had on me, except I grew up feeling that [money] was not exclusively for personal consumption."

Sometimes the Instigators' reflections about family suggested the complex dynamics that mold self-esteem and independence. For example, the two interview excerpts that follow suggest that family circumstances and philosophies converged in positive ways to shape individual talents or to provide special experiences that would later support these women in professional roles. "I was a poor kid who made it, and so I wasn't about to compare myself to men. I was comparing myself to women and finding I was in a great position, where I think the dynamics for middle-class women was to compare themselves to men." "I was encouraged by my family life to be assertive, to get education, to move forward. I didn't have any brothers in my family, there were no sons, and my father was one parent who encouraged his daughters to take math courses, so I guess I had never felt discrimination because I was a woman; at least I hadn't isolated it that way. I attributed most of the discrimination that I had felt to being black. Now I feel that both factors were a part of that."

Parental expectations often reflected the social and economic period in which the Instigators grew up. The Instigators appear to have made some accommodation to those values but at the same time they seem to have been gathering self-confidence and a sense of their direction. For example: "My parents felt that education was the area I should go into. That was still the period. . . . I was not eager to take education, as a matter of fact, and that was a bone of contention in the family. . . . I think it was partly because it was imposed, that it was an expectation, and that for me was a rebellious time. But partly it was because I thought I could do anything and I resented that I was being told that this was an area I should go into, and particularly because they made that clear." "My father wanted me to be a doctor, and I wasted my time because I didn't really like science. But I felt I had to stay with it because it was so important to him, which is a great lesson to me as a parent. I have not done that to my children. So I stayed with it and I handed him my acceptance in medical school and I felt my obligation was finished. . . . I was on fire in college about the lack of opportunities for blacks in white higher education and decided that I wanted to do something about that . . . and on the day I graduated I moved. I went to work at the NAACP. . . . I think my getting on fire was very much a function of my youth in college. I had an intellectual awakening in high school because I was raised basically in a pretty provincial family . . . well off, but with no educational support system."

A few Instigators commented on the influence of females in their immediate families: "I grew up in a family of all women, raised by my grandmother and my mother, and I had two younger

sisters . . . so there were five women. I never had a brother and my
father died when I was eight, and my grandmother was a widow.
In my family, therefore, the word was out that every woman should
know how to take care of herself financially. We didn't think in
those days physically, but we did think financially." "I come from
a family of very strong active women, but they were not achievers
in the sense we think of . . . and I think they were somewhat am-
bivalent. But, they're dynamic, energetic women." "My mother's
father was well-do-to, went bankrupt. My father's father lost his
farm. He became a milkman because he couldn't do anything more.
That grandmother, by the way, was a businesswoman and took care
of all the books and did everything—both my grandmothers ran
their husbands' businesses as the partner and financial manager—
without a title. They kept the books; they took care of the corre-
spondence; they did all those things, and the one grandmother
painted and the other grandmother was an American history buff.
She walked a mile to the library until she was eighty-five, every day
took another book out, and she read some fiction, but it was mostly
straight history by historians."

In the same interview, some family remembrances captured
the essence of family influence on the Instigator—the sense that "to
do" was crucial:

> Each time I had to change my ideas of what I was going to
> be when I grow up—when I had to give up the idea of medical
> school and went to the idea of trying to be a college teacher,
> when I gave up the idea of being an important scholar and
> became a routine administrator—I think I've been sustained
> by the certainty that my grandfather, who went bankrupt, did
> not jump out a window, was not despondent, but carried
> around Rudyard Kipling's "If" in his wallet and rebuilt his
> money so that they could live comfortably and had a new
> beginning.
>
> And I've been sustained by that wonderful sense that
> my mother imparted of transformation. She used to always
> say, whatever age she was, "Well, honey, I wouldn't go back.
> I loved it. I wouldn't have missed a minute of it, but I
> wouldn't go back." Now I think I got from that a sense that

whatever comes next is going to be okay. It won't necessarily be how you think you would have liked it, but it will bring its own special rewards and problems. And somehow that was the philosophy of the family. . . . There was a lot of talk in our family all the time about to whom the Lord gives much, of her will much be expected.

Positional leaders, like the scholars and other researchers, noted the strength and inspiration from parents that the Instigators reported: "My father taught me from the time I was very young that we had a responsibility to everyone in society, and he took me to see the first public housing development in western Pennsylvania. . . . [He] pointed out to me that this was the way government should function, that we should build decent housing for everybody." "I had a very liberal, open-minded, sensible mother and a very liberal, open-minded sensible stepfather who worked very hard in the civil rights movement." "My father was sensitive to people's needs . . . and was very active himself in doing things for workers and their rights."

Not only did these parents serve as role models, they also were very clear as to the expectations they had about their daughters: "[One of the] things that my mother taught me [was] . . . 'be sure that you left the world richer than you found it.' " "I remember my father saying, 'Don't occupy space on this planet. Do something.' " Often these parental expectations about contributing were coupled with strong support of their daughter's personal strengths and intellect. Many of these parents communicated the view that their daughter could do anything she wanted to. When this support came from the father, which was more often the case, it had an even greater impact on the daughter. The importance of paternal endorsement of the daughter's intellectual strengths has been found to facilitate her intellectual achievement as well as her choice of a nontraditional field and a strong career commitment (Astin, 1975).

While most parents played a very instrumental role in instilling a strong value orientation toward justice and human rights and a sense of responsibility to use one's talents and strengths to make a difference, others sent out mixed messages. Achieve, do great things, but also: "[Have] a conventional marriage and settle down in the suburbs."

Such mixed messages and push-pull behavior by parents can have the effect of immobilizing the child, but with our respondents it had the effect of making daughters more self-determined and more autonomous: "I was determined to get away from my family that was very insistent that I make the right sort of marriage, and thus I chose a place that was very far away that I thought they would not come to visit me."

The family origins and backgrounds were powerful developmental agents for the scholars and researchers across the three generational groups. The backgrounds of scholars, for example, reveal three themes as common experiences:

1. *The majority are firstborn.* As a result, they were often adored by parents and grandparents, and hopes and expectations for them to achieve were high on the parental agenda: "I was both the eldest child and the only girl with three brothers. . . . There were no intellectual distinctions on the basis of sex in our upbringing; if anything, more was expected of the firstborn." "I was made to feel very special in [our] household, as the first child, first grandchild, first niece. My father['s] . . . great gift to me was a belief that I could do or be anything I set my mind to." "I was the only child for a long time. . . . I came from a family in which everybody was supposed to do good."

2. While parents, especially the fathers, played an important role, *grandparents were also critical figures.* Referring to her father, one respondent commented that "I wouldn't want to diminish the significance of a powerful male figure in my life." She also recounted the critical role her grandmother played in her upbringing: "I lived with my grandmother. . . . She actively taught me a great deal about assertiveness and power. . . . She consciously told me that I should take second seat to no one, not another woman or man, that I should only allow myself to be in control of what happens to me in the course of my life. In other words, I should depend on no one but myself." To some, grandmothers represented strength and wisdom. Another respondent stated in her autobiography: "My grandmother was beautiful, talented, and much constrained by a patriarchal father-in-law who forbade her, among

other things, to sign the articles she wrote for the local paper. She seized every chance to carry on her education while raising five children. . . . She was one of the few people her son-in-law, my father, admired without reservation. For that reason, and because of elements of the legend which, even as a small child, appealed to me, she has always been a presence in my life. One of my childhood fantasies was that she had not died but had lived to be my guide and friend" (Scott, 1984, p. xviii).

3. *The women scholars had parents who were committed to human rights and social justice*: "I was raised in a household where women's rights were considered to be part of what the rights of people and the rights in society were and I had a father who was adamant about the equal potential and capacity of women." "My father had been a socialist as a young man. . . . My father was a community leader. He was active in politics and also in the Zionist movement." Since they grew up in families where there was a strong social conscience, these women's expectations for achievement and success had to be balanced with a commitment to social justice.

Mentors and Role Models

Role models and mentors give us permission to aspire and to act. We are given permission to be ourselves and to transcend prescribed gender roles. Role models and mentors also inspire us to try to realize our greatest potential.

Mentoring, however, was not part of the common parlance in the Instigator's era, and they offered few illustrations of it. These were women relatively alone in their experiences; they were independent or pioneers by nature—often, a bit ahead of their time.

One Instigator at first strained to classify a male teacher as the "closest I ever had to a mentor," because he provided graduate school recommendations and fairness in teaching women: "If he didn't prefer women, at least he shared everything he had in teaching us and he was rather pleased to have us as students." As for mentoring, or even having a model, she commented: "That was exactly my problem. I had to be my own mentor. There's no question about that, and I functioned very consciously as my own mentor, trying to make decisions as to what would be good for me in the most inhospitable period, with a mother and father who were both proud of me but would be happier if I were married and successful instead of just successful. I did this without any kind of models." "I kept thinking there was a model out there somewhere," another Instigator said, "but there hasn't been a model and there aren't others that have done exactly what we've done."

A male faculty member, however, did evoke a mentor image for one Instigator: "I had a great mentor in college, head of the religion department. . . . He was really a social activist. I took a lot of religion courses just because he was professor of religion and he didn't deal with it in a traditional way at all. He came in with his pockets overflowing with clippings and a sense of indignation about society which I found totally contagious. He was a very important person to me. I guess it was in college that I got a real sense of vision about my life. And [he] was critically important."

Sometimes, searching for mentor/teacher examples produced personal insight for the Instigators, though not necessarily examples of the self-esteem associated with leadership: "The only people I remember clearly in high school, apart from my biology teacher, whom I just loved from a distance and never talked with personally about anything, was the teacher who said she thought I was so marvelous because I didn't have a creative bone in my body, and she was comparing me—I *now* understand—to the most difficult 'A' student one could imagine, and I was a good 'B' student who did everything I was told."

Other recollections of teachers and mentors suggest supportive persons—men and women—though more in the usual academic gatekeeping roles. One Instigator acknowledged a number of women who had helped her, several of whom had served in the traditional position of dean of women and, through that role, had provided early leadership on behalf of women. Recalling one of those women, she said: "It wasn't that she helped me personally but that I saw in her a woman who was very visible and very dramatic, very busy, very important and doing good things." Another teacher "was more of a mentor in terms of my work and of having confidence in me as a student and as a professional." For another Instigator: "The single most important teacher, a man, really sharpened my intellectual faculties and encouraged me to go off to the other end of the world—helped me to put my Fulbright application together."

Similarly, another Instigator commented on the sense of support she had received—less mentoring, perhaps, than simple assistance: "I can think of at least five people who have been extraordinarily helpful to me in terms of teaching me the ways of accomplishing my goals. They were all men. I don't think any of them ever dealt with the issue of women. It was that they were not repelled by the idea of dealing with women. . . . If there was a group of people who really needed some kind of educational assistance, that was just as valid as any other group."

In discussing work assignments, several Instigators referred to learning experiences that sometimes included elements of mentoring relationships. One Instigator, in talking about her role within a college president's staff, recalled that "I learned a tremendous amount and he [the college president] was an individual who, in effect, gave you your head and would back you when you fell down. . . . That was just a phenomenal experience for me, because he had one person who did budgets and one person who did academic personnel, and I did everything else."

Another apprenticeship also involved learning but was a very different kind of experience:

> I did take the job with enthusiasm because I was working for a very top man, an administrator who went on to become [a college president]. I thought I could learn a lot from him and I did learn a lot about administration. . . .
>
> And he did a lot for my ego on a personal basis. . . . He never tried to put any energy into the longer-term career for me. When he left, he neither asked me to go along with him nor did he sit down and work out some future with me.
>
> Like so many able men, he saw me exclusively in terms of his own utility, and was very pleased to have me there as his own person. . . . I learned by watching him, and he liked to unload at the end of the day, tell me what he had been trying to do at that meeting, what he'd been trying to accomplish. He would share with me his reasons for making certain appointments to certain committees, the politics of adminis-

tration. But he did not indicate to me that he thought I had a career ahead. . . .

I did learn a lot from him. But he didn't see me as anything other than a smart undergraduate-type girl. . . . So he was really the tail end of that sexist period. I would say that [he] had a number of conceits. . . . One of them was about brilliant people and one of them was about men, and if I may say so immodestly, I straddled two sets, because I was very smart . . . and I was not a male. In fact, if I could formulate it in more political terms, he probably did see that there were three sexes: There were women, the sort who were dean of the Home Economics School; and there were men, smart men and dumb men; and then there was me and a few special women like me who had no independent careers to look forward to, but who were very much fun to have around.

Sometimes, a male administrator was simply the source of sound advice in accomplishing work goals. One Instigator, when part of a group applying for status as a research unit, was advised by an administrator, "If you want to do research, just *act* like a research unit." For the Instigator, "It was helpful to have someone from his vantage point of power remind me that you don't ask for power, you just take it—you do it—and if it's wrong, someone will tell you."

A fourth work-related illustration is the mentorship one Instigator found in Congresswoman Edith Green's leadership style and behavior. Congresswoman Green sponsored Title IX, the major amendments that extended the Civil Rights Act to cover sex discrimination. As the Instigator recounted it, the process by which Congresswoman Green accomplished this provides examples of learning-by-doing and of the importance of guidance of an experienced hand. According to the Instigator:

There were horror stories we could have pointed to in laying the groundwork for the hearings, but Mrs. Green told us not to. . . . This was the early seventies, women's issues were just coming up, and in the Congress there was not much opposition. People kind of felt, "We'll give the little ladies their due." Mrs. Green told us not to lobby for it. . . . She didn't want anybody to find out what was in it. She was right so we didn't lobby. Mrs. Green was very clever. Instead of having the usual few hundred copies [of the hearings] printed, she got a special request to have about 5,000 or 6,000 copies printed, and they were distributed to every member of Congress with a letter from Mrs. Green. And they were also distributed [elsewhere]. I made up a list of every major educational association and some major libraries and some prestigious people in higher education. So they were really terribly important because they laid the groundwork. They confirmed that sex discrimination existed.

For the next two years, when people would say, "What do you mean [by] sex discrimination?" we'd say, "Listen, the Congress held hearings on this. There are 1,200 pages, documented evidence." And it was extremely helpful to do that because, as you recall, in the early seventies we were crazy if we were interested in women's issues. I think one of the reasons I managed to stay afloat and a lot of people from those days didn't is that I had been legitimized by working on the Hill. In fact, that gave me enormous credibility. Because of that, it would be difficult for someone to say she's a "crazy liberation-type."

The most important role models for the positional leaders in the study were either their parents or their teachers in high school and college. Parents were role models by their own achievement, integrity, and commitment to issues of human rights and justice. For a number of the positional leaders female teachers played very important roles, since so many of them had their early educational experiences in either girls' high schools or women's colleges or both.

These teachers were women with ability and they were in leadership roles themselves, a crucial element to their importance as role models for our respondents: "Most of my teachers, the really good ones, were female, in high school. . . . At the university the great teachers in the department had been females. . . . I had the benefit of some extraordinarily gifted teachers who really cared."

Role modeling is indeed a great teacher; the observation of others whom they admired became an important learning experience for the women in our study. As one woman said, "I take from everybody. I am always looking." Another woman told us how she carefully watched the dean and the president of the institution where she is now the president: "[Both women] set very different models as to how you did the work. I worked for both of them and therefore I watched very carefully. I learned, I think, everything I know about how to do this from watching the two of them."

While our positional leaders talk about their role models, most said they had "no mentors." As one commented: "I've had support [but] mentors . . . not really." For the few who had mentors, their mentors were men: "I must tell you that, in general, I have had no female mentor. . . . I wasn't fortunate enough."

It is not surprising that these women were not mentored by others. While they were developing, in the 1940s and 1950s, there were no women occupying positions influential enough to provide a mentoring role. The faculty in graduate school were men, and, indeed, some of these men did act as mentors. They encouraged our respondents to pursue their own interests, and they provided opportunities for them: "The men were particularly conscious of training women. They believed that it was the women who were going to make it. They gave us good training and opportunities. They gave us a chance to publish."

Women were neither available nor in a position to help mentor or place our study's women in visible or important roles: "And as wonderful as it was to be at a women's college, I cannot say that any of those individuals [women] really shaped me the way the men did later on in my career. Number one, they did not have the power."

Nonetheless there were also some unusual recollections and perspectives about role models and mentoring. One Instigator brought a different perspective to the concept of mentors and models through her remembrance of the Hollywood film influence and its 1950s version of heroines: "I loved those smart-assed, smart-tongued women in movies who ended up editing newspapers and had these male reporters trailing after them with their tongues hanging out. On the other hand, it's a very schizophrenic thing, because while that obviously appealed to something in us, and whoever made it in Hollywood, you know the way those plots always resolved themselves into the traditional role. She gave up the newspaper office for the apron and she got a man and she was happy ever after. And I think that I bought all of it, not just a piece of it. Somehow I never sat down and figured out that you couldn't edit the major newspaper and have the man."

Other Relationships and Roles

The Instigators may not have played out the Hollywood imagery of the 1950s, but they did reflect prevailing cultural expectations in addition to the new opportunities they envisioned for women. They gave examples of both push and pull in their roles as wives, mothers, and leaders. One Instigator offered this view of the demands placed on her as a mother: "I always felt like *the* person that *The Feminine Mystique* was written about, as I'm sure millions of us did. We lived well out of town. There was no public transportation. There was only a highway on which no kid could ride a bicycle so that I provided total chauffeur service for four children who went to four different schools, whose free time and vacations rarely coincided, and who also did the usual Saturday rounds of riding and piano and so forth. One Saturday, I counted it up. It had a slight extra because I also had to pick up somebody at the train who was not on time and I had to go back once, but my total driving for that one day, all in little two- and three-mile spurts, was 250 miles." But several Instigators noted the significant support they received from husbands: "My husband was very, very supportive. . . . He encouraged me to go on and to do, to travel, to do whatever was necessary. He's a very unusual man. . . . He is probably my very best friend; we talked a lot. . . . He would listen to me when I came home and rattled on for an hour before I ever looked up and said, 'How was your day?' It meant a lot. I couldn't have done it without the support." Another Instigator's husband "was very important because he is very politically astute. He's also very supportive of me so that any time I was feeling inadequate (a) I could tell him, and (b) he would brainstorm with me. During this whole thing, he was very important. . . . It's just wonderful to be appreciated."

One Instigator told us how her early family and professional lives worked: "At the time, we had our children. I had no problem with the way my life was arranged. My husband had a job and I taught in the evening, so even though I didn't have a full-time teaching position, the schedule was very flexible. Right from the outset, we decided it needed a three-person support team to have jobs and a child, so we did not have a lot of money. We spent a large proportion giving what we had hiring someone who came in twice a week and did some chores, but mostly took care of [our child], and we always had a three-person support system. I think it's the only way you can do it sanely. And by three people, I mean three people who are willing and ready to do something for that child, because then you've got some flexibility in case one part comes crashing down or there's an emergency." Another acknowledged the importance of both family and friends for support: "When the kids were small, I got a lot of companionship from the children. I think I've also learned something else my mother taught me—that you don't have to be popular, but you need to have friends. I come from a family in which friendship is enormously important, and wherever I have been, I have always made one or two, sometimes a half dozen, good friends and certainly in most places, I've made one or two close friends. . . . If you have family to take care of at home and no household help and a job that requires eighteen hours a day, seven days a week, the friends that you make are going to be the friends of people you meet, on the job. So I never lose my friends. After I have made them, they're my friends forever."

Friendships and other close relationships seem extremely important to the Instigators. Their lives appear to have developed from relatively solo performances—the isolation of graduate study or early homemaking years—to working with a large number of professional alliances and contacts, networks they developed in little more than a decade.

Sometimes, supportive relationships developed within those networks and in the activities the Instigators shared. For example: "For the most part, all of [the women in the network] were involved in the same kinds of things and they were very supportive. On these few occasions when I wasn't getting support from [my husband] either because he was traveling abroad or he just was not able to appreciate whatever fine points there were—women friends were always very, very supportive. . . . The network of friends that I made in those years is still as supportive and friendly as they can be. And I sit over a glass of wine or lunch with somebody that I haven't seen in five years and we're right back with the same level of honesty and exchange of information as before."

Key Experiences

Predisposed to leadership by their heritages, perhaps, or propelled by their special skills and talents, the women leaders also persuasively demonstrate the critical significance of experiences that allow leadership practice. These woman seized opportunities to deal with social issues in new ways, but they were hardly newcomers to the leadership arena. Their accomplishments reflect the integration of previous education, work, and other activities, all of which contributed to their distinctive styles and commitments. Experience frequently provided impetus to their passion and added to their expertise.

Education. The Instigators had in common their formal and extensive academic backgrounds. Well over half hold the doctorate and all completed a graduate program at least through the master's degree. As academic women, presumably they enhanced their leadership with the theoretical underpinnings and academic skills associated with formal higher education. More germane to their leadership, however, may have been the varied experiences they had in both high school and college.

Half of the Instigator cohort graduated from women's colleges. Some talk about institutional character and tone as part of their impetus for leadership and their focus on women's issues. One Instigator for example, recalled, "I had spent a lot of time . . . in a room [that contained] the history of the institution and the history of women's education in America. Whenever I got bored with something I was supposed to be doing I would come in. . . . It really gave me a wonderful sense of the origins of women's education in this country. And if you go back and read that history, it is a history of deep involvement in every major social movement in the country, whether you're talking about the original organization of workers and much of the protective legislation in a whole wide range of areas. . . . The women's colleges had been a part of those social movements, and they've always certainly clearly been in the vanguard of the issues related to women's education. And the faculty had been very active and leaders."

Another Instigator provided a snapshot contrast between her public high school experience and what she found in a women's college: "I was vice president of my graduating class in eighth grade and treasurer of my class for all four years in high school. It was quite clear in those days that the men were the president and vice president, but there were two of us girls who were the secretary and treasurer. [A women's college, however,] . . . provided all those opportunities to be a leader. It was natural. Women were the heads of everything in college."

The college and university presidents echoed the same early leadership roles and experiences: "I was frequently the leader." "I was high school student body president and editor of the high school newspaper." "In high school I was into everything." "In college I was president of my major club." "I was the New England debate champion." "I was in student council." "I think I was president of everything, all the way through school and all the way through college." "I was always president of something, or editor of the student newspaper. I was always running something from elementary school on. I was editor of the student newspaper all the way through."

Some instigators acknowledged leadership experiences in other all-female situations, such as girls' camps and Girl Scouts. One Instigator found important leadership experience as an adult in a cooperative nursery. Prior to the 1960s, she realized, her leadership had been "in all-female situations because women weren't supposed to be leaders when they were with men. I didn't realize it then. It's only when I look back and say, 'My God, I was never a leader in high school or college, because I wanted the boys to like me.' "

Other comments on education often refer to the "solitary" presence of these Instigators in graduate departments—one Instigator dramatically underscores *her* 150–1 graduate school male-female ratio—or the department's distinction as the first major university department to hire a female. The negative consequences of these experiences and of brushes with nepotism rulings will be touched on in Chapter Four.

While their high school and college activities related to leadership development varied, the Instigators emphasized the relationship between early opportunities and subsequent leadership skills, personal awareness, and self-confidence. A few noted the contribution of team sports like field hockey and basketball, and several called attention to speaking opportunities such as debate and theater, activities that offered both leadership practice and public scrutiny. One Instigator with a university career said, "Much of my experience in theater has been as a director, rather than as an actress. I've done some acting and oral interpretation, but my experience, even as an undergraduate, was not as a theater major; I was a history major. But I got involved in the theater program and did direct productions and directed a senior thesis. My first directing experiences had been in my church as a teenager, about fourteen or fifteen years old. So I was accustomed to that. I had been a leader in high school. I had been president of my class a couple of times and that kind of thing. I had been chosen—had gone to Girls State [a leadership program sponsored in all U.S. states] . . . when I was in high school. So I had been in leadership roles I guess throughout [my childhood]." Another woman said that "this [experience of public speaking] started when I was a debater in high school. I can capture the essence, the quintessential idea of something that matters a great deal to me, and that in other circumstances might be considered corny or unintellectual. I can move people." A third Instigator tells us that "I was a theatrical-type child, as many are. I liked memorizing plays and I was in a play, directed plays eventually, was president of a couple of clubs, editor-in-chief of the school newspaper, but never a power kind of leader. I wasn't particularly interested in student government, and not particularly interested either in the authority that comes from office or the authority that comes from power. I rather preferred even to be outside of a main bureaucracy providing ideas that people would glom onto."

Other college activities offered different perspectives and encouraged professional interests or social responsibilities and sensitivities. One Instigator commented that "I was the college's representative to the National Student Association, so I got involved in national student politics, and the very first convention I went to I was elected the regional chairman, and in the second year, vice president." Another example suggests the shaping of leadership through peer models and influences:

> There were Greek sororities which the kids with money joined, and then there were a couple of others. The one that I was in was one of the couple of others and it was sort of the Girl Scouts of [college]. We had jackets and we had our own table in the cafeteria, so there was a place to go in a group where you could feel comfortable and you could always find friends. . . . But it wasn't so much a social sorority. It certainly wasn't connected very much with meeting men or that kind of thing. It was a service sorority, a service to the college. I don't remember how I got into it or how I started that, but I do know that once I got in I was attracted to the people who were in the leadership positions and I was just intrigued— fascinated, I don't know how to describe it. I know that the group of friends I developed in that sorority turned out to be the people who were running it, at least for a certain period, and one in particular was a very charismatic woman. I remember being in awe of her. She had fantastic verbal skills and that kind of charismatic quality to talk and have people respond to her and look up to her and admire her and inspire people. And that's always been there when I think of political women or anybody—that combination of energy and charisma.

Social sororities did play a role in one Instigator's college education. Despite the concern she expressed about their current relevance and appropriateness, she said that "they did teach me, I suspect, something about management and working with people, how to focus on various goals and help people move together as a team to accomplish them."

Student government, theater, debate, sports—these are all activities one might value in leadership development and perhaps assume in some degree to be part of the background of able women. Less predictable are experiences (some in college and others in work and community activities) that involved unusual challenges, apprenticeships, mentorships, and significant role models. The following episode documents such a college experience:

I was chosen to be one of the two people representing [my state] on a major citizenship seminar that occurred in Washington, D.C., and I would say that was one of the big experiences that influenced my thinking about how to educate. There were two of us from each state in the union and we came and lived together in a big house in Washington, D.C., for the summer. We all had jobs in the government that were arranged by the YWCA, which sponsored this. This was the earliest organization to do this. You worked in some government agency in the daytime, then you had seminars in the evening and you learned about your government. I was in the Navy Department with a female boss—who was not given any credit for the brilliant work that she did on organizing ways to use tracking—I believe she was able to use early computer printouts. I never saw the machines, but we would get constant printouts and she was designing the software. She was really building the tracking systems which were very early and very interesting, and I have great regard for her. I could see that this was really masterful. She taught me how to deal with statistics and how to check when things were not appropriate, and to make judgments about the systems that she was designing. She also shared her concern; she had this unreasonably low-level civil service number while all these men had the high titles and the numbers and the salaries.

She was very encouraging about I must do something; I must not go back and simply have children. She was not married. She had no children, and it's interesting that she made that point. At that point, of course, I had been going for a number of years with my husband-to-be and she said, "Whatever you do, don't just settle for marriage and a family. You must do something."

So in the daytime I worked there and then at night we

had leaders in the government speak to us, and it was one place where we were able to eat. We had a couple of black individuals in the group, so no one would have us anywhere in Washington, D.C., except the bus terminal. This was in the early fifties and it was totally segregated, Washington, D.C., our Capitol. It was just incomprehensible. So that was also a very good experience, to be in this interesting mixed group [with] very bright kids from all over the place.

At any rate, the grand thing I think that that did for me was help me see the connection between theory and practice. I heard these delegated heads of the departments. The highest government officials would come and speak at the seminars over dinner. . . . This was really a fabulous program, and it went on for a couple of years run by a woman who was the first female mayor of (I think) Greenbelt, Maryland—maybe the first female mayor in the country. So that's another interesting element. I was very lucky. I was exposed to powerful women who had great mental ability and ability to work with people, and who were doing these interesting things.

Work. Like the out-of-the-ordinary educational experiences, early workplace opportunities also shaped values and influenced career choices. Often, too, workplace opportunities offered at least the validation, if not the development, of certain skills. One Instigator, for example, said that during a college summer, "I was pretty much in charge of one of the stores, and when I was, a lot of energy came out. I started to organize things in a certain way and run some sales, and I did very well with it. . . . I don't see it so much as organizational as I see it is what turns me on, the challenge to do something. If I find myself in a situation and I'm in charge of it, then I get turned on by the challenge . . . really problem solving. I do that all the time. . . . So I had fun doing that, although I wouldn't have admitted it at that time, that summer."

In an even more responsible and risky position was the Instigator who, on her father's death, joined a brother in rescuing a small family business, taking the manufacturing side of the floundering enterprise: "It was exquisite. I was utterly unencumbered by any knowledge or preconceptions and I had the opportunity to move into a failing business where we had not much to lose, and to go systematically from purchasing to production control to negotiating a labor contract with sixteen male shop stewards. . . . I *loved* it, incidentally, because I love the process. I was being measured by whether the business survived or not." She went on to underscore that in her own organizational activities the carryover she valued involved the experience and comprehension of multiple business functions.

A third example of how workplace activities informed later leadership and developed perspectives on women's issues came from a woman who served in a professional organization:

> I didn't really understand how important policy was for women or any other group or cause until I got to [the organization]. . . . I didn't understand that organizations like [it] had an immense effect on policy. . . . I wasn't there very long before I realized that in fact, this kind of organization, which was very much the Establishment as far as I was concerned, could have a lot of leverage. And I now believe that the not-for-profit world, those organizations that are policy oriented are the best single place from which to move national policy, short of being the elected official being responsible in those areas. I really learned from what the men were doing on science policy and research, budget, and things like that. It was not primarily a lobbying arrangement. It was behind the scenes, very low key, knowing who the important Congressional people or staff people were, and knowing people in the federal agencies. That's when we decided you could make enormous strides for women if you went after federal policies: federal policy on research priorities, federal policy on research granting procedures, the makeup of a federal advisory body, the internal rules and regulations and status of women within those agencies. One of the things that we did was to make contact with a network of women working in the federal agencies. They were a source of information; they were a source of complaints; and they heard about us as often as we heard about them. . . . They didn't know leverage. They didn't know what to do, but were a source of information and data.

We were responsible for getting the women and some men—
but there were more women, including minority women—in
those jobs in federal agencies. . . . They were each so isolated
in their own offices in Bethesda or downtown Washington or
out at [an agency], and they learned from each other. Then we
learned from them what kind of pressure to put on the top.
It helped define the role of affirmative action versus the agencies. We learned how to leverage the right Congressional
friends to tap in that kind of situation.

For some Instigators, leadership talents surfaced initially
through volunteer assignments. A college administrator, for example, credited a later foundation grant to her earlier work with the
League of Women Voters: "It was to [the foundation's] credit, I
thought, that they gave me a grant based on my volunteer activities,
because in those days almost no one recognized the value of volunteer work . . . though it was certainly a leadership role . . . including responsibility for a thousand members and a substantial
budget."

Other Activities. The Instigators illustrate an increasingly
common observation about leaders and executives—their willingness and capacity to involve themselves and to learn from experiences. Education and work or volunteer backgrounds cover much
of that leadership development, but some other events surfaced in
the interviews to further drive home the point.

One Instigator emphasized her lifelong active engagement in
sports—her youthful preoccupation with horses, a lot of competitive swimming, and an adult passion for sailing. She commented
that "I spent my youth on a horse, and I had an unusual opportunity to train young horses, which is a very challenging thing. . . .
I think sports were a very important part of my development because I really learned how to extend myself." Another Instigator
broadened her formal education through political and social commitments as an Upward Bound volunteer while in graduate school
and as a political campaign volunteer: "I had the classic experience
of giving up my two weeks vacation to go to New Hampshire, work

for McCarthy, and to sit in a room typing his speeches through earphones."

For a number of Instigators, travel and exposure to other cultures and life-styles shaped commitments and personal skills. For example, a Navy wife who followed her husband's ship to Japan and spent six months there "had a marvelous chance to study women in Japan at that time." That early experience, when she was right out of college, appears to have shaped the perspectives that later led to her work on behalf of women: "I think my experience around the world—having all that consciousness raised about world cultures—having been to Japan, having spent time in Morocco, it was unusual, I think, to be young and have this breadth, to be living in these places long enough to see the subjugation of women. And while we didn't talk about it in those terms, I was obviously digesting all of this in some interesting way."

A similar learning opportunity evolved for another Instigator. Triggered initially through her husband's professional responsibilities, ultimately the opportunity contributed to her own expertise:

One of the things that made me learn to behave more as a professional person happened entirely through my husband because of the fact that [the president of the United States, for whom her husband was working as a science adviser] had his ear to the political ground all the time. And he began to sense that women were going to be important. . . . In the course of that, somehow [the president] picked up the notion that I was a professional, and he began appointing me [with my husband] as a member of these various international groups he sent off to arrange a variety of bilateral-cooperation treaties in science, and to help promote better scientific relations in all kinds of ways.

So I went as a member of a committee, almost all over the world. I didn't go on every trip but we went several times to most of the countries of Western Europe. We went to the Soviet Union, to Japan, South Korea, India, Australia. While my mission on those things tended to be very minor—that is, I was the educational representative who trundled around and actually did the spadework—I found out what it was like for students in those places and for the faculty, and I learned a lot about [what] the context, the texture of university life, or, in some cases high school life, was like in those places.

I learned also that some of the remedies for what was wrong were extraordinarily simple and that they needed somebody like me along who didn't necessarily think that good things could only happen if you start with ten million bucks. . . . Those kinds of contributions became a fairly significant part of some of those missions. It's not what you wrote home about but it made some difference on a local level and, obviously, those things taught me an enormous amount. In fact, I gained a lifetime of sophistication about universities in just those few years of very intensive visits. . . . I know people will say that's not the same as living there for ten years. Obviously not, but you do learn a lot.

Finally, a brief story related by an Instigator that illustrates the risk-taking, action-oriented qualities of many Instigators, and demonstrates how accumulated life experiences build the reservoirs from which leaders draw their strengths and skills:

In 1964, the U.S. government sent me to Malaya to do leadership training of the Malayan women in their villages. Now I have to say that I didn't even know where Malaya was. It was on the eve of it becoming Malaysia . . . and when the telephone rang and the phone caller said, "Would you go to Malaya in ten days and speak to 9,000 women?" I said, "Sure," literally, because I didn't think this was serious, coming out of the blue as it was. But I said, "Of course." And in fact, I did go. In ten days I got a passport. I found out where it was on the map. I didn't have time to go to Washington to be briefed, but they did send me a few thin little pamphlets about the country and I went. That's part of that sense—now it seems unreal—of doing things without knowing the consequences. . . .

It was a stunning experience. As much as anything it made a difference in my life because I found I could do it. I understand the U.S. Embassy did not write an enthusiastic letter about me because I didn't spend much time with them. I spent my time with the Malayans and the Chinese and the Indians who live there, and they were not happy about that. . . . I was taken by a couple of men I never saw before in my life to an Aborigine village, which we had to crawl over tree trunks and all those kinds of things just to get into, and they showed me how they made their poison darts and so forth. . . . There were eleven women in national organizations, and what the government really wanted was for me not only to speak, but to help the women to write a national document that would bind their organizations together into one consortium. And we did that.

What emerges from these reflections and from the accounts of our other respondents are consistently positive recollections about family interactions, admired role models, and challenging encounters in school, work, and travel. These experiences clearly helped to encourage and shape the development of leadership interests and talents among our three generations of women leaders.

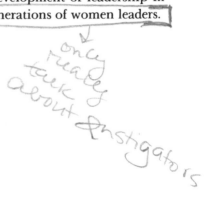

only really talk about Instigators

CHAPTER 4

The Common Thread: A Passion for Justice and Social Change

> There is a torch. I think the torch has to do with
> making it possible for women to be what they can, and
> to me, that's what it's about.
>
> —*Inheritor*

In this chapter, we capture insights from the women leaders' personal stories that help us achieve a greater understanding of the dynamics of leadership. What becomes clear here is that leaders emerge from the critical interplay of personal values and commitments, special circumstances or historical influences, and personal events that motivate and mobilize people's actions.

Values that stand out among the study's women are a passion for justice and social change and a commitment to women, or, as we identify it here, a feminist perspective. All three generations describe the role historical events (for example, the Depression, World War II, and the civil rights movement) played in shaping their experiences and values. Thus, historical influences are a powerful force that shapes leader behavior. Personal experiences also play a powerful role in shaping core values that motivate people to act.

Once again, the center of our analysis is the Instigator cohort. What drove the Instigators' passion for change and distinguished their leadership? What gave them the urgency and capacity to put ideas into action? We also give attention to the Inheritors because so many of them described, quite eloquently, how historical influences such as the civil rights movement and the new left shaped their commitments. In addition, we look at the positional leaders (for example, college presidents or foundation officers) and nonpositional leaders (for example, scholars) to note that the sources of their leadership are strikingly similar.

A Passion for Social Change

Almost universally, the Instigators shared a vigorous commitment to social justice and change. They were veterans of numerous social movements and causes—labor, peace, civil rights, antiwar, wages, housing, jobs, education. And their involvement began early in their lives. As a high school student, for example, one woman had campaigned for the minimum wage in Massachusetts. Another, who described her participation in interracial high school dances in a community of segregated schools, also recalled her later confrontation with discriminatory land-purchasing policies against Asians in the Berkeley, California, area, and her eventual involvement as a white faculty member in a predominantly African-American school.

Another Instigator recalled, "I was on fire in college about the lack of opportunities for blacks in white higher education and decided I wanted to do something about that." That early "fire" led to work with the NAACP and eventually to her launching of a national fellowship service to help place African-American students in predominantly white colleges and universities. She elaborated on her commitment to social justice as follows: "I have had a clear vision of what I perceive to be two very critical problems in our society. One is, I really had a clear sense that I didn't want things to be the way they were—for blacks, back in 1945, in terms of education, or for women back in 1962 or before both of those periods. I really thought that it was wrong for blacks and for society and for women and for society. I didn't think the women's situation was good for women or for men. I really believe in creating options, making it possible for people to do what they really want to do. I didn't think every black had to go to a white college. I just wanted

them to have access. I didn't think every white or black had to go
to college. I wanted them to have more opportunities. . . . I believe
that options can be achieved by making it work for everybody. I feel
that every social problem lends itself to that. The only thing that
varies is the timeline." Another Instigator said of her college years:
"My major interests were civil rights, so even though I had leadership roles in college, for example, I was not very interested in the
activities of the sororities. I was probably one of the few people
among the people I knew—my friends, my classmates—who participated vigorously in the early civil rights movement in the early
fifties. I was a member of CORE . . . and I went in the summer to
Washington, D.C., and I worked for the Friends Service Committee.
Right behind the Capitol were all these slums. . . . It was amazing.
We used to track the railroads. We had tar and we had our little tools
to make the windows close and the doors work. We did a lot of
physical things. And then we picketed and carried signs and tried
to get desegregation to occur in Washington in the early fifties."

A third woman explained, "My orientation and training, if
you wish, for the women's movement came from the civil rights
movement. . . . I really think I understood race relations and conflict and discrimination personally, for the first time, when I lived
in Asia. . . . I just experienced firsthand what discrimination and
racial attitudes had meant in those countries. . . . Later on in that
decade, I met women who had discovered that there was something
called sexism, women who had never noticed there was something
called racism. And it surprised me because I just assumed that those
went together."

For one Instigator who did civil rights work in the South, the
contrast between her life as a Northern woman and the lives of her
Southern sisters was instructive: "The civil rights women, the ones
who had been brave and opened their homes to the Freedom Riders
and the sit-in people in the early sixties, were completely ostracized
from their communities. Their churches threw them out, their parents wouldn't see them, and they were thrown out by their husbands, and I was struck with how different it was from the North.
If you took a political position that was antiestablishment, you paid
a very high price as a woman in the South. In the North, I sensed,
as a Northern woman, I was permitted to play with politics as an

aside, never having to draw the personal severe consequences of my political activities. And that's a very profound observation to make. . . . I think it's the first time I thought about women as a political and social category. . . . In my experience, our politics was just a game. And my mother, I'm sure, harbored the hope throughout this period of activity that I would find a doctor in Scarsdale and settle down and this would be just a part of my memories, my extended adolescence."

Peace dominated the early thoughts of another Instigator:

By the time I got to be a senior in college, I took some courses in political science. I took a course in international politics and I took another course in the United Nations. I was very, very interested, as so many of us were in those days. For you have to know that it took me years when I got to this country to be able to hear a plane flying overhead without being frightened. I spent a lot of time in air raid shelters in England, so I still had that. And I grew up in a house where the dinner table talk was all about my father's family. They were all shot one night in a village in Poland. A lot of that was just with me as part of my growing up. So I was interested—if you would ask me then, if you could do anything more that you're interested in, my response would have been peace, world peace. In those days I thought that had to mean world government.

So I graduated from college in January, [I] pounded the pavement looking for a job, and the first place I went was to the United Nations. And I went there to apply for a job because I wanted to work in the service of peace and I wanted to offer myself to the United Nations. I wasn't aware of women's issues or feminism or anything at that point. But I went and I did this at the U.N., and they told me what I should do if I wanted to work at the U.N. was to go home, practice my typing skills, and come back and apply for a job in the secretariat as a secretary. So that was my U.N. experience. I didn't want to do that. I wanted to be an ambassador because that was how I could go to another country on behalf of the United States, that was how I could make world peace. I wanted to make a difference. I've always said that. In fact, just the other day, people were introducing each other in a group, telling about how they knew each other, and one of the things that somebody said about me was that I had told her some years ago—and she'd always remembered it, because she is a child of Holocaust survivors and I am a survivor myself—what I had said to her was that I believed that you could have your professional life and your personal life, that personal politics and your profession work together.

The Instigators appeared to bring to women's concerns not only a sense of justice but also their capacity to conceptualize, to generate ideas, to see the "bigger picture," and to seize opportunities to elevate their ideas into tangible formats or operations. In a number of instances, they described themselves as visualizers: "I was the leader, because it was my idea. And I had the clear vision. When I have ideas they come to me in structures. They're completely clear from the beginning, and it always seems to me it takes months, sometimes years, to explain them to other people. And I'm willing to do that because I believe in political action." This Instigator went on to describe how her vision shaped one of the early conference efforts on behalf of women: "It's hard to believe I was so innocent, but I really concocted in my mind the idea that this subject [the feminist perspective] was worth exploring, that it would bring community people and graduates together. . . . I would take the bus up on Friday nights with a whole bunch of other girls going up to see their engineering boyfriends, and I know that I was struck with the self-inhibition, the self-effacement, the dependency . . . of these young women, and while I didn't identify with them, quite, because I was a grown-up . . . I'm sure that contributed to my thinking. But it was '68. The antiwar movement was over. I had suffered this discrimination and the sense of impotence in that movement that a lot of other women felt, and here I had the opportunity to run this conference."

Another Instigator voiced concerns that generated a focus on the urgency of research on women: "I was extremely upset with the lack of activity, concern, and involvement of the women's colleges, particularly the Seven Sisters, in the civil rights movement of the

1960s. . . . It seemed to me that if those institutions did not look at themselves in the context of women's needs and concerns, there wasn't any point in the continuation of the Seven Sisters. . . . I think the conceptualization [of a research center] is really in many ways my own approach to questions related to women's education and questions related to women in the marketplace. How do you do the basic research on the pedagogy of women's education and how do you get that translated back into the classroom? The women's colleges had been successful. What is it in their approach to education that can be translated to a coed surrounding?"

One respondent provided a case history of how ideas and the talent to envision help to mold organizations and social structures. It is worth retelling her story in some detail. What we know today as the College for Human Services in New York City traces its roots to a mother of two small children in the 1950s who had some concerns, ideas, and needs of her own: "I wanted to do something intellectually and I wanted to raise children. . . . Then I decided I had to do something challenging and interesting, so I thought I would like to form an organization that would help women like me who had the intellectual ability to do something in the research and writing area, but who also wanted to take care of their young children."

In 1957, with a partner in the Washington area, this Instigator developed a social science research organization to provide corporations and government agencies with part-time women researchers:

I began to build a pretty decent research organization, and we had some publicity. So I received thousands of résumés. I was inundated. Women heard about it, sent in their résumés, wanting to work for us. I mean the button we had pushed in terms of need was absolutely enormous. . . . So I think I'm a social inventor. I see a problem, then I form the organization to solve it. I think very early on I became a practical political scientist. I began to see it's almost like the cyclical ideas of economic theory when you are trying to work on making something happen in society, social change. If you're going to hang in there, you're going to go through a certain cyclical process. First, you are going to come at it, and then you're going to be rejected, but you're not going to go back all the way. You're certainly going to try again. There is a continuum of pressure that you have to put on the system. You have to keep making changes that hopefully do not ever tamper with the basic integrity of what you're trying to do. But one has to make political adjustments so that the system accepts this entity. Something has to be done to negotiate out the differences, and then you can move again, make a little more progress.

Next the organization moved to New York and underwent a transformation:

What happened was a very natural transition. My partner decided that she was going to continue to have children and did not want to continue to work at Part-Time Research Associates because it was just too demanding, and it also was in New York—obviously a much better place from which to do Part-Time Research Associates, at least at that time, because the corporation's headquarters were here.

Then I spent the summer codifying the résumés that were coming in and feeling so heartbroken, realizing that I could not hire all these individuals. I had categorized their backgrounds, and I realized that they'd been in traditional categories. All I knew at the time was, oh my God, another teacher, another nurse, what am I going to do? I cannot hire these people. I had built a very good client base, but I didn't have enough to make use of the thousands of talented women who had been sending me their résumés. . . . At any rate, I said to myself, first of all, this is a growing big business, and I have to make a choice. Am I going to build a business or am I going to solve the women's problem? I knew this was the major course that had started Part-Time Research Associates, yet I was beginning to become a businesswoman. Then I wondered if there were some way to connect my civil rights experiences with all these women who were sending me résumés. And that kept bothering me. . . . I was putting all these women, these résumés, into a file and never touching it. So I said, maybe there's some way to have these women who are teachers and social workers help low-income women. If we could pull them together, if I could figure out a way, then maybe I could hire many, many women and give many women jobs.

And what I started to do at that point was try to figure out jobs that teachers could *train* people for, and social workers could *train* people for . . . and it was really just a glimmer of an idea first. Maybe those teachers could train low-income women to be something like them. While these low-income women are working in the school system, they learn and grow from the professionals and become teachers themselves. Maybe we could do the same thing in the health field and in other areas.

That was the beginning of what was really [a form of] professional education, and it was for women, low-income women. That was called the Women's Talent Corps, and I incorporated that and I gave it that name. This was 1964 that I founded Women's Talent Corps. At that point, the Economic Opportunity Act was passed and it was clear that there were going to be dollars to do some work with the Corps. And so I said, well, I will figure out a way to design several new jobs above entry-level—there were people who helped in the schools and there were hospital attendants—I figured maybe there was a job which did not exist at the time. So I started running around the city of New York and it became a passion to find people out there who would let some people come in and work there in new positions. In the daytime I approached hundreds. I guess the time it took me to get this funded was over the years, '64 to '66, maybe two and a half years, actually. I met hundreds of community leaders, trying to build a base of some kind of support, told them my idea for an education that would go with these jobs, and that we could move [people] up on the basis of performance, that if we could slowly make the connection between competence in one's work and education that we would be able to bring a lot of people into the work force.

In 1970, the fledgling College for Human Services earned the right to award the Associate in Arts degree and to become a full-fledged college of New York State. From the part-time research business to the federally supported Women's Talent Corps to the designation of "paraprofessionals" in the teaching, health, and legal fields, this Instigator had turned her values and her vision into an institution.

The passion and vision that characterized the Instigators also moved and energized the positional leaders (the college and university presidents and foundation officers). Their passion for justice and human rights, for improving people's lives, and for changing institutions became the central themes of their stories: "I cared passionately about the concept of legal rights for women. . . . The only thing that keeps you going, if you are a genuine person and committed, is that you care." "I care a lot about the cause that I had been a leader in."

Historical Influences

Forces that shape leader behavior represent the internal drive of values, and the capacity to forge direction. Leadership also reflects the influences of history. The Depression and World War II, for example, toughened the women who lived through these periods and generated courage to resist and not succumb. These times also sensitized our respondents to a plethora of injustices, not the least of which includes gender inequality.

The Depression took its toll on the families of the Instigators: "The grim decade of the Depression had begun. . . . The deeper the family slipped into hard times, the more my father drank and the less we had to eat. My mother skipped lunches, and became a janitor in a four-family building, shoveling coal into a greedy furnace, lugging a dozen cans of ashes up treacherous stone steps twice a week. The men did not have enough work and women had too much work" (Rossi, 1983, p. 7).

Other historical periods such as the Suffrage movement were singled out by some of the women Predecessors. One Predecessor told us that she was taught by teachers who were suffragists. Born in 1903, she was in school during the suffrage movement. "My high school teachers were feminists . . . Feminism in those days was suffrage. That was the women's issue."

The impact of history is particularly vivid and relevant if we look clearly at our most recent leader cohort, the Inheritors. They are the women who were in college during the 1960s, a time of great unrest. They were the participants in the civil rights and anti-Vietnam demonstrations. They were the first generation of African-American women to have experienced busing and they were among the first few blacks to have entered white colleges and universities.

For those Inheritors who are academic scholars the civil rights movement by their report seems to have had an enormous impact. Direct experiences in militant organizations like the Black Panthers and participation in the Vietnam War protests taught them lessons and fueled their quest for social justice: "I was always a political activist—[starting with] the nuclear test ban treaty in the '60s. . . . In college, I was involved in civil rights and anti-Vietnam war protests." "I got caught up in this sort of social consciousness state, then racial awareness. . . . I began to hear things because my friends and I would go to the rallies and to moratoriums." "I've been a radical all my life . . . for fifteen years or more, a social radical of antiracist movements. I was engaged in the civil rights movement before there was a civil rights movement."

World War II and the oppression associated with it were experienced directly by one of the scholar leaders, who said poignantly: "I grew up as a Jew in a fascist, Catholic country. I grew up as an antifascist in a fascist country. I was in the underground student movement as a teenager. I survived Hitler. I was in jail at the age of eighteen. If I knew nothing [else], I knew how to resist . . . I think that there is an important connection between my work as a historian and the fact that I am a refugee. To me, the decisive experience was the refugee and the Holocaust experience, and the fact that I lived through that and I lived through the policies and events leading up to it made a decisive impact on my work—and on everything: on my life, on who I am."

Personal Experiences: Toward a Feminist Perspective

The Instigators' passionate activity on behalf of women reflected their basic belief in justice and equity, but their convictions, or even a feminist commitment, developed quite individually. Sometimes the development was intense and sudden, at other times it was gradual, and often it came with nagging reluctance. Indeed they were leaders—skillful, influential, energetic—but their efforts on behalf of women represented a variety of perspectives.

As activists, the Instigators—whether in leadership positions or as academic scholars—sharpened their commitment to social justice and learned the power of protest for bringing about change. Their passion for justice was also fueled by their personal experience of discrimination, rejection, belittlement, and pain as women. All of these experiences impressed on them the need for knowledge that could be central to changing social institutions.

Although all the women in our study took active roles in the 1960s and 1970s, their perspectives, their approaches, and their pace differed. Sometimes they vacillated between philosophies or goals. For many, it was difficult, in those early days, to recognize or identify with top issues. About her gradual adoption of a feminist perspective, one Instigator commented, "I wasn't angered, because in some ways marriage, in some ways the graduate school career, in some ways the kind of childhood I never had . . . despite problems, I'd always manage to do what I wanted to do. Now, I may not have had visions and dreams of things that were impossible. Maybe I'm such that I accommodated myself or there were some limitations that I processed out—anything I might have wanted to have done that wasn't available for women."

Another Instigator, who also did not immediately recognize the effects of sexism even on her own life, suggested that negative experiences may have made her more receptive to feminism later on:

In graduate school, I had no feminist consciousness but I do remember very clearly that the issue that kept coming up from the professors, because of the two of us, my husband and myself, both being in the same graduate department, was well, what are you two going to do about your jobs? You won't both get hired. That came up and I don't remember . . . I don't remember at all being angry about it. I don't remember at all thinking this is unjust, let's fight it. It was just, oh, husbands and wives don't get hired in the same department and I understood why, because oh, well, one couldn't vote on the other and it would be complicated if one did well and the other didn't do well, and so on and so forth. Nepotism in a department.

Then the other thing that came up a couple of times was the question about competition, and I can only tell you I had no experience of competition between us. . . . I attributed my unhappiness that first year to the transition from childhood to adult life. We'd left school and got to the first job. I attributed it to hating [the city] and I attributed it to being seen as a faculty wife. I had spent six years being an equal graduate student with him, doing very well, and suddenly not only was I invited to pour tea—these people didn't know my academic background—but I'd find myself at these receptions and parties given for new faculty introducing him into the faculty community, and I would find myself having the experience of being invisible at his elbow. . . . Here I had been just teaching my courses, professors, everything the same, and suddenly I was invisible at his elbow, and suddenly I was asked to pour tea. I found myself being placed in a role, in a position which I had never prepared myself for, did not attract me in any way, and I found it offensive that they did not know who I was. I was the graduate student working on a dissertation on Herman Melville and they ought to know, and they ought not [to] be seeing me as Mrs. Assistant Professor. I know that a lot of that fed into and prepared me, made me ripe, for later responses. But it was a bad experience. I disliked it intensely.

Though many Instigators reported experiences like the previous one, they were not necessarily attracted to the women's movement right away. One respondent gave the following explanation for her resistance: "The women's movement was coming very much on the heels of civil rights, the black movement, and there was a lot of suspicion, and I was among those who were suspicious, that it was a way of co-opting the energies of that movement. It took us a while to realize some of the factors of history, that this was a repeat essentially of the abolitionists' period and suffragette movement and so on, but I was concerned that my energies would be drained off from a struggle that I thought was very important. But I decided that I would go to the women's center . . . if I could possibly use its resources as a means of including the concerns of women of color, though not exclusively that. I did not want to be designated as the black representative, but just to try to ensure that it be an inclusive effort." Another woman described her reluctance to become involved with the women's movement this way: "I was a token woman in a male organization that was concerned with civil rights, peace, and sort of improvement of college life since we were all academics, and I had absolutely no sense of myself until I went to that first series of . . . official meetings, no sense of myself as a person with a mission. I certainly didn't really want to work on the status of women. I wasn't convinced that it was a terrible problem except for a few people who were going that way anyway. I didn't see the whole picture that early."

Still another Instigator noted that her feminist consciousness developed slowly. As a married graduate teaching assistant who was faced with nepotism rules, she said, "I really sort of took it as 'This is the way the world goes and how do you cope within the world,' rather than 'How do you fundamentally change the rules?'" After getting her degree, publishing, and spending three years as the only woman in her department, however, she became more attuned to feminism: "You add these things together along with a rising consciousness of the way the world has to be and I think all of those things add up to saying you were truly interested in the women's movement."

Whether their identification with issues affecting women was gradual or rapid, whether they see their actions on behalf of women, in their own words, "not as extreme feminist" or as "radicalized," the Instigators in this study contributed the basis of what we now talk about as the second wave of the women's movement.

Although the details vary, the Inheritors told essentially the same story about the development of their feminist consciousness as did the Instigators: "The message came across real clear. When I would go to these meetings (Panthers or NAACP), I would raise my hand and say something. There would be silence. . . . Fifteen minutes later, a brother would stand up and . . . arrive at the same thing I had arrived at, reword it a little bit [and people would respond,]

'Yeah man, oh yeah.' Well, that only had to happen a few times before I understood—not that he was bad and I was good, but that what was going on was that women could be brilliant, but you had to give your idea to a man."

Discrimination at the institutional level was a common experience: "The institution in which I was first appointed . . . provided a great deal of support for my husband in the summer, and the idea was that in the summer he was to do his scholarly work and the equivalent assumption was that in the summer I was supposed to take care of the baby." "My husband and I ran into a serious nepotism problem. . . . The dean, who is now dead and who was at that time chief officer, essentially said I should go home where I belonged." "In an odd way there were not a lot of expectations for women. . . . I came to Harvard with a degree from Swarthmore, so you could have thought there would have been great expectations about what I was going to do. There were none. . . . Harvard thought that taking women students was a joke, sort of. It was said publicly. We take women students to keep our junior faculty happy. . . . 'They're going to have children and it's a waste of our time to train these people,' was their assumption."

Her early experience of discrimination, coupled with her being an outsider—that is, teaching in an untenurable position—for a while, gave one woman the freedom as well as the impetus to pursue her feminist scholarly interests:

> I was outside the field, so I wasn't trying to get tenure, and I wasn't bound by their methods. . . . It was only then [when I saw this] that I realized that these theories had been built from all-male samples, and I was stunned, first of all, about this design flaw. A psychologist building theory from an all-male sample? I was stunned. I was equally stunned by the fact that I had . . . taught this stuff before and I never even noticed. . . . This was in the 1970s and the movement had started, and this was certainly in a context when to raise such questions one didn't come up against the kind of stone wall that I would have ten years earlier. . . . I saw a problem. . . . I was cued to see it. . . . It had a lot to do with my academic, intellectual training. But what I saw, what made it possible for me to be

heard when I spoke, was the women's movement. There is no question [that] two strings of my life came together, my academic and my political interests.

Another respondent assessed a painful two-year tenure struggle in another institution as indicative of what women were generally experiencing then on the faculties of colleges and universities. "I describe it as a pathology in which nothing a woman can do would be enough. . . . It wasn't just me. It was happening all across the board. Any untenured woman who came up was being treated this way and we knew it because there were only 100 of us [women] on the faculty. We knew what was happening." As a result of that experience, she has taken on the role of an outspoken advocate for women at her current institution: "The commitment is based on the fact that, as a tenured woman, I have the responsibility to stand out in the cold and be a voice because there are so many women who cannot. . . . Once having earned the security of tenure it is not sufficient for me to hide out and seek my own success . . . without providing the kind of shelter I can, trying to create the kind of climate that will not make that so difficult for the next person. . . . There are small things one can do that in some respects have an impact that's useful. So one thing I did when I first got here was to read the graduate catalogue, and when the language was sex-biased, I listed it out and sent the dean of the graduate school a memo about it." She sees her leadership role not as a person in a formal position but as someone who is "articulating a set of issues to women as well as to men in the university and trying to set up the issues in such a way that they will get serious consideration and trying to encourage other women to speak out, to organize, to become a power, to shape their own fate."

While discrimination could have diminished the spirit of these women and even silenced them, instead negative experiences energized them: "I underwent the painful experience of being fired by an anthropologist when he saw a good thing in a study I designed and fielded. . . . It was my first consciously defined experience with sex discrimination, and it began a slow burn that gathered momentum and was gradually transmuted into a first feminist publication" (Rossi, 1983, p. 11).

What were some of the early influences on positional leaders that instilled in these women a sense of mission or caring and the desire to make a difference? As we suggested in Chapter Three, it was probably a combination of family background (where there was a strong emphasis on human rights and on the need for social activism) and their own victimization as women and/or as members of minority groups that made these women leaders. Encounters with discrimination and other kinds of injustice—especially during their formative years—played a key role for the positional leaders in the study. For some, it had to do with the contrast between early educational experiences in girls' high schools and women's colleges, where they did not encounter discrimination, and later experiences in coeducational environments, where they witnessed or experienced a considerable degree of sexism. One woman became aware of discrimination when, after her high school and college years in women's institutions, she became a graduate student and later a young faculty instructor at a Southern university: "I had my first job in a coeducational institution, which was very discriminatory about everybody, and I guess I was the only woman who really knew down deep inside that it did not have to be that way . . . I started fussing . . . I began to say, 'Why are we sitting here accepting this nonsense?' . . . There were two kinds of nonsense: one was that you had at least three women who were in arts and sciences, I was the fourth. They had never had a sabbatical. They had never risen above the associate professor level. They had never been department chairmen; at least in two cases they were the most distinguished scholars in their departments and they just moused in and taught their courses and were beloved by their students and moused out." Her second observation had to do with students. She saw how good the work of her women students was but how unwilling they were to speak in class: "I would say to my students, 'You're writing the best papers in the class. It would be very good if you would share some of your thoughts with the rest of us.' . . . All the students that dealt with me there were men, and that began to suddenly ring bells for me since I had not been in coeducational class as a student." Very early on, this woman saw how the system silenced the women students in the classroom and the women faculty at the institution. The early experiences for her were also coupled with seeing the

injustices inflicted on African-Americans: "The other thing they
did at that place [was] they didn't let black people eat in any of the
little joints in the town or stay in the dormitory." Thus, she set out
to be an activist. "I worked very hard with civil rights issues. . . .
We opened up all those eating places, and we opened up the
dormitories."

Another respondent recalled discriminatory experiences both
at the university and after graduation: "Graduating from the university, I ran into a lot of discrimination and so I had my consciousness raised about that very early on." This woman, born and raised
on a different continent, recounts her early awareness that women
in her country were not able to get foreign service or other government jobs. As a high school student, she attended an all-girls' board-
ing school with high academic standards: "It was the kind of high
school where 70 percent of its students pursued university education." But equitable treatment at the university was not available
for both genders: "I was the only woman who [became part of the
small, elite honors program]. Nobody from my school or anywhere
around in my age group did that. . . . Lots of black people report
that experiences of discrimination are really crushing. I was crushed
that I couldn't get into any of the prestigious occupations that I
personally wanted to contribute to in my country."

Yet another perspective comes from those women whose influence and whose leadership flourished in the world of ideas. What
prompted the women scholars—nonpositional leaders—to undertake research and writing on the topic of women? What helped them
decide to shift from the traditional paradigms in their discipline
into new ways of seeing history, of understanding human behavior,
and of analyzing the social system? Like the Instigators and positional leaders, these women are characterized by an acute awareness
of injustice in our society. This awareness is the direct result of
personal experiences—experiences they have had in the family and
in their schools.

The women scholars and researchers spoke clearly about how
they have integrated their scholarly interests with their social activism—how and why they use scholarship as the vehicle for transforming social institutions. They are interested in the study of
"women's lives and experiences that could be used as the basis for

reconsidering existing institutions, structures, and assumptions," as one scholar put it. They have chosen to engage in scholarly activity about women out of a desire to bring about change. "[I] wanted to do something to improve the situation of women in society." "I thought of [my book] as a contribution to clarifying the record." "I wanted to see women get a chance in a very generalized way." They are social innovators, and their research and scholarship represent their social activism: "My real activism has been my research." "I feel productive work is the creation of knowledge, and I guess the end result of productive knowledge is increased understanding that benefits the quality of life." "What I really want to do is to start letting my work speak more for me. . . . It is very important to sort of leave a legacy." This last scholar's comment refers to her work on African-American women. She has come to feel that writing about the lives of women of color will have a more pervasive effect than only speaking about them which reflects the belief these women share in the power of scholarly research and publishing.

This chapter has underscored both the unity and the diversity of the core Instigator group, the women across our three generational groups who filled leadership positions in institutions, and women whose leadership flowed from their scholarly pens and platforms. All shared the commitment to justice and social change on behalf of women. Their motivation stemmed from different historical and social contexts, and frequently from painful personal experience. What we learn about leadership from these women are the critical elements: values that address change, the energy of personal motivation and involvement—whether from positive or negative experiences—and the capacity to look up from oneself and out to a society and the future. Woven together, these powerful forces coalesced as second-wave feminism.

CHAPTER 5

Leadership for Change: Initiatives and Outcomes

> I really measure my life by the extent to which I can
> help to effect change.
>
> *—Instigator*

Leadership studies are about people, but they are also about outcomes, an important construct in the conceptual model described in the first chapter. In identifying the Instigator cohort— women leaders who were instrumental in bringing about changes on behalf of women from the mid 1960s to the mid 1970s—we looked for specific women who:

- Conceptualized women's situations—hopes, needs and frustrations—in this relatively uncertain, ambiguous period
- Created new life patterns and opportunities for themselves and others
- Dealt with the problems and frustrations of institutional change
- Provided training and mentorship for the Inheritors, women who would come after them

We knew what the Instigators had accomplished—this was how we had identified them as Instigators in the first place—but we had few of the details or an accurate chronology of their accomplishments. We also knew relatively little about how these leaders went about their activities and even less about their origins, early experiences, and personal lives.

This chapter is about the accomplishments and results of the Instigators' leadership. We employ their recollections to map the initiatives they took. We look at the triggering events and the individual twists and turns they engineered or endured. In their interviews, we hear what one might expect of any phenomenon as complex as the women's movement and its relationship to social change.

Leadership Initiatives

The Instigators' initiatives on behalf of women covered here span slightly more than one decade, from the early 1960s to the mid 1970s. We offer a partial list of programs, organizations, and activities initiated by them. Although there is some overlap among Instigators and among these initiatives, the list is chronological, beginning with the founding of Catalyst:

> Catalyst (1962)
> Continuing education programs for women (1958 and early 1960s)
> Women's Talent Corps (1964)
> MIT symposium "Women and the Scientific Professions" (1964)
> Women's studies (1969)
> Caucuses, committees of the academic disciplines (1969)
> Executive Order 11246 (1969)
> Feminist Press (1970)
> Center for the American Woman and Politics (Eagleton Institute, Rutgers University) (1971)
> U.S. Office of Education, National Summer Institutes on Affirmative Action (1971)
> Project on the Status and Education of Women (Association of American Colleges) (1971)
> Centers for research on women (1972)
> Committee for Concerns of Women in New England Colleges and Universities (1972)

Federation of Organizations for Professional Women (1972)
HEW affirmative action regulations (1972)
Title IX (1972)
Office for Women in Higher Education (American Council
    on Education) (1973)
Women's resource centers (1973)
Signs (1975)
National Council for Research on Women (1983)

In one form or another, each of these initiatives remains as part of our educational and social landscape. Some have celebrated milestones of twenty or twenty-five years.

Our interviews provided clarity and chronology for these initiatives; they also underscored the complexities of attributing leadership to a particular person, because frequently the 1960s produced collective, collaborative efforts by and for women. Instigators often acknowledged the pioneering thoughts and energies of others who had helped them succeed or had laid the groundwork for their labors. Sometimes the interviews revealed the simplicity of what women were trying to do; they were not always trying to make major changes, to move mountains. Overall, it could be said that the Instigators focused attention and created formats and structures to fit the needs of women in a period of considerable social, political, and economic unrest. Sometimes the needs were as straightforward as finding ways to finance continuing education. Often the Instigators involved themselves in more than one initiative or joined together to ensure success. Sometimes they moved in and out of institutions or positions to promote their ideas, and sometimes they worked alone, especially when their own personal experience pressed them to act. Their accomplishments—the outcomes—enable us to appreciate not only the magnitude of what happened in a relatively short period of social history, but also to relish the creativity, passion, and productivity of the women responsible.

The initiatives we describe as part of the study fall into five general categories: (1) programs, policies, or units within higher education institutions; (2) groups and coalitions in the broader academic community; (3) organizations peripheral to academia but focused on the educational needs and backgrounds of women;

(4) publishing and other means of distributing information; and (5) legislation and national policy. The first part of the chapter describes the initiatives that represent the changes these leaders were able to accomplish, and the second part analyzes the events that triggered actions that led to these changes.

Initiatives Within Higher Education Institutions. Among the first efforts on behalf of women, the continuing education programs—sometimes called reentry programs—appeared as early as 1958 in a few experimental models, specifically at Radcliffe, Sarah Lawrence, and the University of Minnesota. By the 1960s, several colleges and universities had followed suit, adapting the models or developing new approaches to fit their assessments of local and regional needs. Although each was designed to fit a particular institution, the centers and programs nonetheless promoted missions similar to this one, from the University of Michigan: "to help women enter and stay in the mainstream in higher education and professional preparation and to help the university respond to their special needs, that is, to attend to issues of equity and to lower the institutional barriers to the equal participation of women" (Van't Hul, 1984, p. 1).

Almost simultaneously, women's concerns and issues forced academic institutions to offer broader services and resources to address different female constituencies. This affected faculty, staff, undergraduate cohorts without family responsibilities, counseling and career services, health and child care. In some instances, efforts became formal structures, women's centers or resource centers. In other cases, they developed as policy committees or commissions on the status of women.

One of the most visible and significant contributions of the Instigators dealt with the core of academic institutions, the curriculum and research. Women's studies, an interdisciplinary field that recognizes the significance of women's history and experiences, found a receptive though cautious audience in an initial 1969 conference. From one or perhaps two identifiable formal programs, the field has grown to about 500 programs today, and the field maintains visibility and momentum through its own national association.

Soon after the curriculum changes associated with women's

studies, centers and institutes for research on women appeared.
Early formal centers at Radcliffe, Wellesley, and Stanford, for
example, as well as the Center for the American Woman and Politics (CAWP) at Rutgers, encouraged such an expansion in research
activities that by the early 1980s these organizations formed their
own coordinating body, the National Council for Research on
Women, with sixty-five members to date.

Often, distinctions in the objectives of women's centers
blurred as they met demands across constituencies to offer services,
courses, and research. The following description suggests, in more
specific terms, the crossovers of purpose and activity that the early
centers experienced:

> I had inherited a concept that I believed in, and that was a
> center as an umbrella organization and one in which all
> women could be a part. It would be a vehicle for various
> groups on the campus. And that meant that it could include
> lesbian concerns but would not alienate those women who
> were not a part of that particular thrust. I guess one of the
> metaphors I used in those early days was that the center could
> choose to go out like a meteor, and there's some validity to
> that. I don't knock that concept, but we must be clear about
> the choices we make. It could do that, go out in a great flame
> of glory, because it had taken on some major issue and kind
> of gone down the tubes with that or we could opt for an
> organization that would be here for a period of time. And I
> opted for the latter, but it was a clear choice. A bit of every-
> thing quite honestly. We took on issues like child care, which
> meant participating on certain kinds of committees when a
> letter of support was needed providing that. Sometimes only
> brainstorming and strategy sessions with people were neces-
> sary, and when it was advantageous to the cause—to whatever
> cause, like child care—for us to show up, we would show up,
> and know how to work effectively with that particular issue.
>
> One area that we worked with and developed into a
> kind of major program was faculty development, which was
> really a way to help assistant professors, women assistant pro-
> fessors, get through the tenure process. We coordinated the

program with the faculty center and we then were able to ensure that certain issues of affirmative action, the problems that women and minorities face, were not just injected into the dialogue there but were a real part of it.

We also thought it was important to have the young male faculty present because at some point they would be in the position to make certain kinds of decisions. So it started out as a program for women assistant professors, and the very next year all of us decided that we should open it up but still maintain the integrity of the program. So that was one way we worked with faculty. . . . Now that's the visible program that we did, and coaching—meaning that we did through this program try to make it as clear as possible what the process was, what people's rights were—because that's not something that is clearly articulated on this campus and many others like this campus.

It's all kind of secret and if you don't have the right mentor who is in the right place and knows the information, you won't ever find out what it is all about. What you should be doing, at what point you should do this, what kinds of strategies others had worked out, what was successful and not successful strategies and all of that kind of thing. So it seems to have worked its way into the institution as something valuable for the Women's Center to be involved in.

The Wider Academic Community. Instigators catapulted many of their ideas and issues into regional and national forums. In the academic disciplines and professions, for example, caucuses, committees, and commissions elevated women's concerns for equality, particularly for professional career options. By 1972, sufficient numbers of such groups existed to warrant another umbrella organization, the Federation of Organizations for Professional Women, with its purpose being to link various women's committees and caucuses of the professional associations. In 1972-73, a survey of fifty-two groups revealed that rosters in the associations listed over 38,000 professional women. (A list printed by the American Association of University Women in 1973 included seventy-six women's caucuses.)

In the higher education associations, leadership for women focused on special offices, projects, and advisory bodies, the latter having both male and female membership. In 1971, for example, the Association of American Colleges undertook its Project on the Status and Education of Women. Its goal was to collect and distribute information about women for administrators, faculty, students, government, and educational and professional organizations. Though originally proposed as a two-year study, the project is ongoing and today lists 100 original papers to its credit. In some years, it handles 20,000 requests for materials and mails its quarterly newsletter to as many as 17,000.

The American Council on Education (ACE) opened its office of Women in Higher Education in 1973 with the mandate "to improve opportunities associated with American colleges and universities." With ACE's Commission on Women, the office was to address national issues affecting women and to suggest approaches and solutions as well as policy statements.

A final example of initiatives in the larger academic community is Higher Education Resource Services (HERS). Its introductory statement to "HERStory," an article that appeared in *Grants Magazine* in 1978, captures some of the essence of our Instigators: "Lots of people have good ideas. Translating those ideas into action, whatever the field—research, social programs, creative work of all kinds—is another matter. It takes planning, design, organization, hard work, clear presentation, and finally money. The story of HERS—Higher Education Resource Services—is the story of an idea which grew into a useful functioning organization through the dedicated efforts of a small number of people committed to making equal opportunity for women in academe a reality" (Hornig, 1978, p. 36).

HERS represents the visions and strategies of several women administrators who met informally as the "Committee for the Concerns of Women in New England Colleges and Universities" (known thereafter as the "Concerns Committee"). In response to the pressures for affirmative action on campuses, and the reliance of colleges and universities on recommendations from the few women in higher education posts, the Concerns Committee proposed HERS, a registry and referral service for women who possessed credentials for faculty and administrative positions. Initial funding for a two-year project opened HERS in 1972 as a talent bank with services for referral, academic career advising, and consultation with institutions about their affirmative action plans and procedures. Two decades later, HERS continues to serve the higher education community and includes various spin-offs, particularly HERS-Mid-Atlantic, formed in 1974, which developed the national Summer Institute for Women in Higher Education Administration (now in its second decade).

Organizations Peripheral to Academia. Although there are numerous examples not covered in this study, initiatives that focused on the talents and needs of educated women for recognition and roles in the workplace played a significant part in shaping the women's movement and changing institutions. The Center for the American Woman and Politics, acknowledged earlier as a women's research center, is both an organization within a university and one with a distinct focus to design and sponsor programs "aimed at developing and disseminating knowledge about women's political participation." Since 1971, the Center for the American Woman and Politics has convened conferences and forums for women legislators, provided research on political candidacies and populations, and systematically collected and distributed facts and figures on women in politics and government.

Catalyst, another organization, responded early to what its quarter-century report calls "unprecedented social change." In 1962, with an initial board of five college presidents, Catalyst's Instigator/founder launched an effort to be a "facilitator of a process that would address the frustration of women who had not established their careers before taking time off to rear children, and the waste of their talent and training after the children grew up and left home" (Schwartz, 1986, p. 2).

In its initial years, with grant support, the independent, not-for-profit organization promoted the feasibility and advantages of part-time employment in the public sector, particularly in public welfare and teaching. Over twenty-five years later, Catalyst functions as an organization designed to "help employers identify the high performers and take whatever steps are necessary to clear their path to the top. We can also aid employers as they formulate policies and practices to help working parents balance career and family" (Schwartz, 1987, p. 3).

The Women's Talent Corps is a third illustration of an independent women's organization, which evolved into an academic institution later on—the College of Human Services. The Talent Corps was organized in 1964, and its roots reflect the same ferment and frustration of women searching for a place in the changing workplace.

Publishing and Other Means of Information Dissemination.
Vehicles for distributing information became crucial to the success of most efforts on behalf of women. Facts, figures, issues statements, and policy recommendations claimed much energy and the bulk of modest budgets for many of the organizations just cited. Two initiatives deserve special mention. The Feminist Press took off in early 1970 as the intersection between evolving women's studies programs and the need for a publication arm that could print syllabi and distribute materials to a new cadre of people who wanted to teach about women. *Signs* followed in 1975 as a scholarly journal to publish new scholarship about women throughout the world with an interdisciplinary emphasis. In the first editorial of that journal, the editors talked of the "new scholarship" as follows: "What is novel is the amount of intellectual energy men and women are now spending on such scholarship and the consciousness that often frames their efforts. That charged, restless consciousness respects many of the concepts, tools, and techniques of modern study. It uses them to compensate for old intellectual evasions and errors, to amass fresh data, and to generate new concepts, tools, and techniques. It also tends to question the social, political, economic, cultural, and psychological arrangements that have governed relations between males and females, that have defined femininity and masculinity. It even suspects that those arrangements have been a source of the errors that must be corrected" (Stimpson, Burstyn, Stanton, and Whisler, 1975, p. vi).

Legislation and National Policy. In 1970, actions on behalf of women accelerated when federal legislation demanded compliance by colleges and universities with standards of equal employ-ment opportunity. Executive Order 11246, issued in 1969, provided urgency, authority, and visibility to women's issues when the order's application to sex discrimination was ferreted out—the work of an Instigator. Another Instigator later offered this interpretation: "The addition of the word "sex" to the list of prescribed categories in the 1964 Civil Rights Act was accomplished by one woman, working on behalf of the then newly established Women's Equity Action League (WEAL), who read the fine print of Executive Order 11246 as amended in 1969. Everything that has happened on the campuses since then has had its origins in that insight and in that action."

On the heels of the Executive Order 11246 suits, the Department of Health, Education, and Welfare's guidelines on affirmative action ordered employers—for example, colleges and universities—to establish affirmative action programs for women as well as minority groups. The issuance of those guidelines incorporated the efforts of many women who had assumed leadership throughout the decade of the 1960s and thrust many more women into campus leadership roles to implement federal policies.

In 1972, a major piece of legislation followed: Title IX of the Education Amendments. It was designed to extend efforts to end gender discrimination in institutions of higher education. Title IX reads in part: "No person in the United States shall, on the basis of sex, be excluded from participation in, be denied the benefits of, or be subjected to discrimination under any program or activity receiving federal financial assistance."

Again, the legislation represented the initiatives and energies of women leaders, often in association with male supporters, and the successful lobbying efforts spurred them to take further steps to address women's concerns.

In identifiable ways, Instigators who served as leaders in the types of initiatives described earlier shaped the climate for women over the past two decades. Their accomplishments generate some observations:

- The outcomes represent structures, formats, and approaches that didn't exist previously; the Instigators made things happen—organizations, institutions, networks, talent banks, positions, language, legislation.

- Flexibility and adaptability were crucial in translating ideas across constituencies, geography, and institutions, frequently in the face of limited or no funds.
- The initiatives in which they took leadership roles underscore the reality that things don't "just happen"; leadership involved vision, energy, support, collaboration and, frequently, crucial triggering events or circumstances.

Triggering Events

Like the proverbial peeling of the onion, recitation of these initiatives on behalf of women reveals the complexity of what really took place in the era of the Instigators' early activity on behalf of women. Interviews offered further insights into how and why some Instigators stepped into leadership roles, and what sparked their actions.

Illustrative is the following series of recollections by the woman instigator of Executive Order 11246, as amended to cover women on college campuses. The scenario begins with the Instigator's personal and painful recognition of discrimination in her own life in academia. While pursuing graduate work as a wife and mother she considered women as a possible research topic, only to hear her adviser respond, "Well, women—that's not research." Her reaction fit her sense that at the time "I was not really interested in women's *issues,* that I knew of. So I didn't see that as discrimination. I saw it as an individual instance of [my adviser] being difficult." However, the problems she encountered in her search for a job later on prompted her to ask a faculty colleague why she was not being hired. His observation: "Well, let's face it. You come on too strong for a woman." Her response: "I went home and thought about how I had come on too strong and I started to cry." Her husband, on the other hand, voiced his sympathetic assessment: "That's discrimination." A third incident involved an application and interview for a research position, "for which I was well qualified." The whole interview evolved into the employment interviewer's discourse, "Well, I don't want to hire women because . . . ," which eventually led her to an employment agency where "the guy looked at my credentials and said, 'You're not a professional. You're a housewife who went back to school.' "

These different experiences set in motion a significant search for activities on behalf of women that she described as follows:

> Those three incidents really had made me think more, and it occurred to me no matter how good I was, I would never get ahead if there was such a thing as discrimination. I got involved in the Women's Equity Action League, because they seemed very nice and conservative. At that point I thought NOW was much too radical because they picketed occasionally, and that was something *I* wouldn't have done.
>
> I read an article in the newspaper about WEAL and got in touch with them. I was naive enough to think that if something was immoral, like sex discrimination, it should be illegal. So I started reading up on it, not that I was going to file charges. I don't think I had anything like that in my head at that point, but I just wanted to know that it was illegal I guess to make myself feel better, and found out quickly that it was not illegal. Then I made the decision that I would find out how blacks had done it.
>
> At that point I was naive enough, too, to think that the blacks had solved all their problems, which obviously they haven't, and hadn't, either. But I began to read up on discrimination of blacks in schools to see if there was something there that was relevant to what women could do. I had no idea where this would lead me. I don't think I had anything in mind.

She continued to describe experiences that reflected her *discovery* of legislative weapons with which to fight discrimination against women:

> I was reading a booklet from the Civil Rights Commission which talked about civil rights, [by] which they really meant minority civil rights, and they talked about this Executive Order which prohibited contractors from discriminating in

employment on the basis of race, color, and national origin
and religion. There was a footnote, and being an academic I
read the footnote and it says this order was amended to cover
sex discrimination effective October '69, and I screamed. That
would have been in the fall of '69. So I made the connection
immediately that universities had federal contracts, therefore
universities were prohibited from discrimination.

At that point there were literally no laws that prohibited sex discrimination in education. Title VII excluded educational institutions and their educational activities so that
employees were not covered. The Equal Pay Act exempted
executive administrators and professionals, so, again, faculty
were not covered and Title VI of the Civil Rights Act only
covered race and national origin. So there were no laws pro-
hibiting discrimination against women in education. By the
time I discovered the Executive Order's application, I was
ready, I guess, to do something. My first reaction was, I'm

probably not reading this accurately. It probably doesn't cover
women, sex is covered, but I'm probably not reading it right.
But then it's not unusual for women to not trust themselves.
And so I called up the Office of Federal Contract Compliance,
the Department of Labor which enforces this Act, and asked
if it covered sex discrimination. And the woman put me
through to the head of the Office of Federal Contract Compliance and he said yes, it did, and he'd like me to come down
and talk with him. . . .

So I went down. He was the head of the Office of Federal Contract Compliance and was very eager to have someone
do something about sex discrimination. So he grabbed on to
me. He was extremely helpful. I went in very nervous because
I had never talked to a government official before really, but
he was genuine. He wanted to do something about sex discrimination. I think he cared about discrimination. He was a
white male, as a matter of fact. I believe he was the one who
suggested that we file a charge, and I didn't know anything
about filing a charge.

And she proceeded to describe the activities that resulted in the necessary legislative changes:

> But we talked about it, and you don't have to be a lawyer to file a charge because it's a charge with the government; it's not a lawsuit. He helped frame the charge, he helped devise the initial strategy to get it done. For example, he said you've got to have some documentation. You've got to have a lot of papers to go with this class action charge. And I said there's nothing written on sex discrimination, because I had been looking for it. And he said, well you've got to get something because you've got to have a lot of paper to convince people. They're not going to read it anyway, but you've got to have something so people will think there's something going on. So I began looking and found two studies at two institutions and I did a quick and dirty one at my institution, not telling them what I was doing but going around from department to department saying I was doing some research and getting some information. So we had three studies about three campuses. We were just looking for the pattern of discrimination that the higher the rank, the fewer the women, that women were not being hired in numbers anything like their availability.
>
> For example, I was able to find data that said women were 23 percent of the doctorates in psychology. And what happened was you'd look at the institution and they had, maybe, one woman at that point in their department—considerably less than 23 percent. So we were able to make the case on that basis. I didn't know what a charge of discrimination should look like. So he helped frame it. We got WEAL to file the charge. He suggested that we send copies to key congressmen.
>
> WEAL was a little nervous about my doing it because they weren't quite sure whether this was really going to be embarrassing to them. Finally, they reluctantly allowed me to go ahead and use WEAL's name. And they gave me a fancy title. I was the Chair of WEAL's Action Committee for Contract Compliance. The whole committee was me. The presi-

dent of WEAL felt that if you had a fancy title it would be better. So I was the whole committee.

[The government official] suggested that we send copies to congressmen, which we did, and he said they don't have to take sides on a complaint. What you do is ask them to write the Secretary of Labor asking that the government enforce its own Executive Order. That's all you're asking for. I sent a little note to key congressmen. . . . We had eighty pages of material by the time I was finished. Some of it was just statements saying women are not treated well on campus. A staff member at [a foundation]—this goes way back—Xeroxed (we had no budget) 100 copies of the eighty pages and sent them down to me. So we had 100 copies of the eighty pages and then I excerpted four pages from that, which we could afford to Xerox and we sent that off to the congressmen, and said, please write the Secretary of Labor asking him to enforce his own regulations and orders.

Well, because I also sent copies to the press, the word got out that there was a way to file sex discrimination complaints, and we began to get information. And we didn't need too much information. I would tell people to give me the number of women and men and percentages in each rank in psychology, music, English, and a couple of other departments and then we would be able to say, well at Dismal Swamp University there's a disgusting pattern of sex discrimination in the department of X, and we'd give the national availability figures. And then I'd say, okay, now this is [whatever university it is], you give me this information and I'll file it with my name signed to it, but you've got to get as many women as you can to write your two senators and your congressmen and ask them to write to the Secretary of Labor, and also the Secretary of HEW because there was joint responsibility. And we generated so much congressional mail that, I think it was HEW, they had to put somebody on full time just to answer the congressional mail. . . .

This was a very good issue because we weren't asking the congressmen to vote. We weren't asking them to say there is sex discrimination at your state university or there isn't. We

were just saying this is an issue and please ask that the government enforce its own regulations. This is a nice neutral one.
So it didn't matter really whether you were conservative or
liberal, you could write that letter and you could tell your
constituents that I have, indeed, written the Secretary asking
that he will look into this matter as soon as possible. It was
very, very helpful to do that because congressional letters are
important. They get answered. There's a special person in
every department who handles them. And the letter goes up
and down the department in a special folder, and everybody
reads the original letter from the congressman and then everybody reads the response because somebody low down [in rank]
writes the answer and then it goes up and gets signed off on
[by the congressman].

So we were sensitizing people in the Executive Branch
about sex discrimination in education. And we did the same
thing on the Hill. What this did is it made me an instant
expert on something nobody was an expert at, which is a way
you can move ahead, really rapidly, because nobody in higher
education knew the Executive Order except me. Literally.
They didn't know what it was. I think I filed the first charges
at the end of January 1970; by March or April investigators
were on the campus of Harvard and Michigan. . . . As a matter
of fact, those were two charges I didn't file. It was the group
in Michigan that had filed the charges and I had given them
a lot of help telling them how to frame it, what to write, what
kind of data to get. So they had done it. And I had done the
same thing with people at Harvard. The NOW group in Bos-
ton filed charges there and I had given them a lot of advice on
how you file charges. I think I filed about 250 charges by the
time I was finished.

From these comments, it is clear how one Instigator's personal experiences provoked the actions that led to major legislative
influence in the Executive Order and Title IX legislation that
followed.

The development of the *Feminist Press,* another major initiative, traces its roots to the cry for syllabi for the emerging aca-

demic courses focusing on women in the late 1960s. The Instigator
who was the founder of the Feminist Press recounted a phone
conversation with a distant colleague, also an Instigator, in which
they acknowledged the intensity of demands for the syllabi they had
developed or collected. At one point in the conversation the colleague said, "Well, let's do it. Come [here] for a weekend and my
secretary will type the syllabi." As the Instigator remembers: "Of
course, I type, too. The three of us typed like mad and we did it.
It was incredible. I can't tell you how many nights I didn't get to
sleep over that foolish thing." Once typed, the syllabi were photo-
graphed and Know, Inc., a woman's printing and distributing organization in Pittsburgh, assumed final production responsibility.
That was the origin of the Feminist Press.

Similar urgency triggered the evolution of HERS, which, as
we have described, was the offspring of the equally inventive Committee for the Concerns of Women in New England Colleges and
Universities. The latter began as a retreat of female senior administrators in predominantly male institutions, "very consciously to
give us an opportunity to let our hair down, exchange notes and
also to have some kind of power base or communication base vis-
à-vis the men."

As another Concerns Initiator described the group, they met
regularly to talk about common problems, learn from one another,
see what they could do for women in their respective schools, address pressures they were beginning to experience, and identify and
recommend qualified women for administrative and faculty positions: "All of us were interested in how you could provide a clear-
inghouse, how we could know about other women, and minority
women as well as white women, who were available. Before we were
searching for people, it was always so hard to find where the talent
was, and we came up with this idea of having a spin-off organization that would be the resource for all colleges and universities who
were looking for qualified women."

Thus, HERS derived its first challenge and direction from
the Concerns' insights and pressures. One woman in a leadership
role at that time conveyed the message she was getting from male
colleagues: "Find me another gal as bright as you are, and I would
hire her on your recommendation." Whatever the language used,

the challenges offered an opportunity not to be missed. Women in new administrative positions themselves, carrying names and addresses around with them, hoped such activity could be regularized by running their own placement service.

Another significant stimulus for leadership and initiative was the vehicle of conferences and national or regional meetings that focused attention on women's issues. The 1964 symposium at the Massachusetts Institute of Technology, for example, brought together men and women to discuss problems faced by women in science and engineering professions. The welcoming remarks of the president suggested the changing climate of American society: "A conference at MIT on science and engineering is hardly a novelty; but a symposium about women on a campus that very likely you thought to be a man's preserve, may well have appeared to you as something remarkable" (Stratton, 1965, p. XI).

In 1971, the U.S. Office of Education sponsored a training institute, "Crisis: Women in Higher Education," at the University of Pittsburgh. Designed "to develop models for aiding administrators and faculty in the identification of patterns of discrimination, and the development of appropriate strategies and programs for Affirmative Action and institutional change," the initial effort promoted a national network of three institutes at the University of Florida, the University of California at Irvine, and the University of Tennessee ("Challenge: Women in Higher Education," 1972, p. 2). Program components in the seven-day institutes included topics identified as crucial to equal educational opportunities for women: Affirmative Action, Women's Studies, Research, Socialization and Sex Role Stereotyping, the Women's Movement, Minority Women, Junior Colleges, Child Care, and Continuing Education.

Beyond focusing attention on women's needs, concerns, and issues, conferences provided women with new opportunities for affiliation, collaboration, and leadership. They offered platforms for leaders to gain visibility and confidence in themselves and their ideas and to test their ingenuity and persistence. A 1969 conference at Cornell University proved to be a critical event for women's studies and other women's initiatives. This Instigator's account offers a picture of the genesis of such a conference as well as the impact these events had:

It was a period when there was some experimentation with the calendar and Cornell was going to try 4-1-4 and have an interterm, and my job was to solicit ideas for programs from various members of the faculty, coordinate, do up a little catalogue, then hope that students would come back. I discovered, not surprisingly, that nobody was ready to put himself or herself out for a course until they knew for sure that the students would be back. So on my own I came up with the idea that what the administration should do is sponsor one or more large events that would guarantee some students would be back and then go out to the faculty and say, "We're pretty sure we'll have a thousand students or 500, let's see what you can offer." In that spirit I thought through a conference idea on women. I met Kate Millett early on, saw her whole theory . . . and I invited her to participate in this conference, along with Betty Friedan.

And then another relevant development occurred which taught me a great lesson. I had generated some money for the conference because the dean had invited one of the "old girls," by no means a new feminist, but at least a member of the older community of women activists, to speak, and he was afraid there would be no audience for her. And so my having a conference of which her speech would be one event was appealing to him, and he offered us the thousand dollars or so we needed to bring up Millett and Friedan and organize a conference. By then I'd already touched bases with a few interesting people so I was developing a core of people. I hooked up a collaborative committee to plan it, and had the experience which I've since had many times—going around and asking if anyone was interested in this, and one thing led to another.

We were a group of 30 women, graduate students and staff, with one or two faculty women, who planned the Cornell Conference on Women for January 1969. There were so few faculty women at that time. There were 1,400 members of the faculty of which 100 were women, of which 75 were in the College of Home Economics. There were 25 women distributed over all the other fields. Well, I had gone ahead and done a fairly radical program, radical means going to the roots. So instead of having sessions on women and jobs, women and education, the first session was called, "How Do Men Look at Women and How Do Women Look at Themselves?", which was getting in on a very profound level of image and self-image. The second was, "Is the Woman Question a Political Question?", which generated a lot of hostility from the new lefties on campus who thought this was all marginal to politics. From then on we dealt with abortion, we dealt with lesbianism, we dealt with issues that only five or ten years later would become mainstream issues..

We set up panel discussions of our male social scientists treating these subjects, as it turned out, debating the new feminists. Since they had had no way of knowing who the new feminists were or what they would talk about, they were ill-prepared for the debate. . . . We're talking about something that had only been emerging for the last twenty-four months. As a result, the social scientists brought with them all their traditional contempt and superciliousness in regard to these issues, their lack of knowledge and their lack of embarrassment about their lack of knowledge. It was quite a jousting match. They were really done in. Two years later they never would have participated in such a meeting, but they were totally caught by surprise.

A month before the meeting took place, the dean announced that he wasn't sure he could fund this conference. I believe he didn't like the way it was evolving, and I experienced my first Kafka-like barrier, because what he was saying wasn't "We won't fund it"—that would have been an issue—but "We might not be able to fund it." And if you tell somebody that a month before the conference, it is enough to kill the conference. I suppose my first radical, feminist action was to go back to that committee of 30 and say to them that I was prepared to put $500 toward that $1,000 budget if, from the remaining 29, we could raise the additional $500. I thought we were being had by this bureaucrat and the only way to deal with him was to simply say we were prepared to raise the funds to go ahead with the planning. If he couldn't fund it, that would be just too bad.

I called Kate Millett—we were going to pay her way by
air—and said, "Is there any way you can rent a car and drive
up?" Each of these accommodations radicalized the conference
even more. Everybody visiting the conference stayed in the
same house. That meant that we rapped until 3:00 in the
morning during that conference, that it became a much more
intense, intimate experience. So this dean's decision was one
of the lucky phenomena. In the end he did pay, but it was also
very significant for us women to sit there and look at each
other, most of them married, and most of them socialized to
take any of their savings and put it into either their children's
welfare or buy themselves a fur coat to make their husband
look better and say, "Yes, I can give $75" in 1968 dollars to
make sure that this thing does happen. It glued our commitment to one another.

The conference was scheduled for a room seating 90
and we had to move immediately to a room that seated 400.
We think 2,000 individual people came to that conference. It
went on for four days. There were four sessions a day. Nothing
else was going on on campus because of interterm, and it was
just for 2,000 people, it was the click experience, and when you
have 2,000 people clicking, it's a roar. So it was quite spectac-
ular. And, of course, we identified in the audience another
concentric group beyond our 30 planners. People from the
audience would speak as articulately and as penetratingly as
the people on the platform, so that it was not only exciting
to watch the debate and watch the men get taken on, but it was
also exhilarating to find sister intellects around. Everywhere
you looked people would be looking up and say, "Who's talking? Who is that person? I never knew she existed." Also, it
was just the experience of being in a majority. There were men
at the conference, but by far the women were the majority.

Recalling their earliest efforts, the Instigators described the
creation of a culture and a climate. In some instances, they defined
true start-up endeavors where the risks were unknown, experience
was lacking, and timing was crucial. Time and again, they also

reminded us of the necessity of political savvy and sensitivity to one's environment.

Elsewhere we describe the personal setbacks and challenges the Instigators faced. However, their recollections about these initiatives clearly document their collective efforts and the mutual support that reinforced their inclinations and stimulated their creativity: "There was a community of people there, and a lot of what became part of the feminist movement came out of there. I think maybe there was something in the air. . . . Primitive forms of our bibliographies that we used for teaching [were produced at Know, Inc.]. . . . [It was] almost like a cell, and a lot of people and a lot of activity came out of there."

Meetings and conferences provided platforms for women Instigators and enlarged their networks for communicating ideas and sharing materials. Networking among colleagues—and more intense feelings of being colleagues—offered support to the Instigators both within their own organization and across groups: "When I was faced with having to put together an agenda, I asked what other organizations in town were doing and I made contact with any staff person I could identify around town."

Constituencies appeared to lend Instigators support and to help broker issues. The culture of the second phase of the women's movement emerged early as one of collective support and shared responsibility and credit for success: "The four of us (two women who chaired the advisory committee) formed a four-person team that created the center in its first two or three years. . . . We worked together. I came in with a proposal and a budget, [and] the cochairs suggested, 'You should always make a budget larger than you need. That way you can leave room for negotiations.' They told me how to double the budgets. . . . They were the ones who knew about foundations and corporations and government and politics. I was the academic one."

In this chapter we have chronicled the events, accomplishments, and changes that we and others attribute to our initial Instigator cohort. These Instigators, through their actions, have pioneered landmark events that describe and define the second wave of the women's movement. They have been the instigators of major legislation enacted to combat sex discrimination in education, and they have been the creators of women's studies and the new scholarship. They have created a climate of action and through their passion, vision, and social agenda for women they have changed our institutions and the way we think about gender arrangements and the social construction of reality.

CHAPTER 6

Key Skills and Strategies of Leaders

> As an empowerer, I really think that the highs for me have been making people do things they could never do before. Giving them the confidence and the criticism and the help and the ideas, and sharing my *chutzpah*, the *chutzpah* I was born with, and making them have it, too. So that's the empowerment.
>
> —*Instigator*

The experiences and accomplishments that propelled the Instigators to act reveal only part of the picture. Learning about their strategies and leadership styles enriches our understanding of the special dynamics that made them agents of social change. Beneath common motives and perspectives rests a range of skills and experiences. Knowledge of that background challenges myths about women's leadership and encourages recognition of diverse leadership styles and new approaches for the recruitment and development of future leadership talent.

While a major focus of this chapter is on the Instigators— the women who accomplished major institutional and legal changes on behalf of women as described in the previous chapter, we also attend to the styles and strategies of the positional and nonpositional leaders. We do so in order to depict further how women's leadership empowers others and mobilizes a collective action toward the common good. We also extend the concept of leadership beyond position, as our conceptual framework argues that leadership can be positional as well as nonpositional.

Special Skills of the Instigators

The earlier descriptions of the Instigators' accomplishments suggested some common skills and talents, particularly their action orientation and organizational expertise. In interviews about their activities on behalf of women, leaders talk about being prepared on issues, reading about and listening to what was happening in their environment in the social context of the 1960s, and internalizing and understanding "the usefulness of very long and even boring meetings that go on forever, and having the patience to hear everybody out." Another Instigator said about the "general stirring" of the decade and some of the early efforts to reach out to women: "I read about those things and started a little private file. I was interested, and I began to think . . . [that] 'none of us had any power individually.' When you put it all together, we had a lot of power and the reason was we had a lot of information and we had one another."

We have already alluded to the Instigators' capacity to be inventive and to take risks. Their own words call attention to these qualities: "I'm a futurist enough to always look ahead. I'm always looking to see what the next steps will be—what's new in the environment or what's coming down the way that somebody is going to need to know more about. . . . I think it's been an enormous help to spend a lot of time reading and thinking and putting together this array of things that are out there in the environment, seeing something that's moving, that's happening. . . . I think I got to be much more of a leader by being inventive and creative and risk-taking than by any other single set of adjectives you might string together—those things which help you to explore what's new and make you willing to point the way to what's new." Another Instigator recalled the risk and innovation in the early development of women's studies courses. In some ways her comments demonstrate the freedom to be creative and to take risks if you are not a total insider to the system:

> The course evolved very organically as we came up with a tentative list of topics and then presented each other with what would be a lecture say, in capsule form, and then opened it for debate and discussion. So we were already innovating in terms of style. We were collective. We were not hierarchic. Since all of us were underemployed, how could any of us rely on our status to lord it over the other? . . . This seminar was a bag-lunch seminar. . . . We were willy-nilly inventing the style of doing business that would become appropriate to feminist politics and women's studies. . . . I can't imagine many professors allowing their work to be presented in a tentative fashion to their colleagues and being as open to criticism and change as we were. . . . When we taught the course . . . we sat in on everybody's lecture. We didn't just pop in and out like stars, but we would sit in on the lecture being given, and comment from the floor, so the students had an opportunity to watch rather sophisticated people as peers deal with complex issues. . . . The next action I took that I think was full of radical implications, was to advertise the course once it was approved. It wasn't in the catalogue, of course, but in the student newspaper, and I got tons of calls the next day telling me in what bad taste it was to advertise a new course. I paid $35 for a display ad, and I agreed with them that it was bad taste but we managed to get 200 students enrolled.

 Ingenuity frequently complemented political astuteness. The Instigator just quoted emphasized the ability to understand and use the system: "The way we got a course launched . . . was to get a professor who was out of sorts with that same department . . . to sponsor the course. In other words, we played the elite university's procedures against itself. Being an elite university, they had tremendous confidence in their faculty, and if a faculty member took responsibility for a course, it would sail through curriculum approval committees." She ended her anecdote by making the point that the introduction of a large lecture course "created a constituency."

The experience of another Instigator left a similar imprint: "We had to work out a strategy of kind of softening the system up a little bit at all levels . . . and I guess one of the things I learned was that this is a political process and it doesn't matter who's right or wrong. What matters is how much you can get your way."

The Instigators also demonstrated the ability to make good use of networks, which have been crucial to their leadership contributions. One Instigator provided this illustration:

> You talk about my involvement in the national circles and what that meant. The people on this campus did not know [person's name]. I had met her through the networks and knew of her work and read materials that she'd written and so on. And we had been discussing strategizing on this campus with other women, investing in some office. We planned that whole encounter, everything in terms of having her interact with the faculty and the chancellor. She gave a visible public lecture. That was the reason that we brought her, but the most important things she did were to meet with the chancellor and to speak to a luncheon of key people on this campus. As a result of that visit, we then had the impetus here. It took us two years to get a position which we still have. . . . Now that was a direct contact, you see, and there are many other examples of that, I'm sure. Other women have other examples also, but that was a way in which we were able to use what we discovered through the national networks to the benefit of the campus.

Our interviews revealed other skills the Instigators brought to the challenges they accepted—for example, their adeptness at using forms of communication, such as writing, as critical strategies: "You turn an idea into an event . . . the way of making it happen in reality. A conference, I think, is one form of an event. . . . So that is my most obvious strategy: to make it happen in front of people. . . . Now the limit of that is you can't make it happen in forty different locations, so you have to write about it, then, so people who aren't observing the event can observe it vicariously." Another Instigator described her modus operandi this way:

I went around to all the faculty members who had wives who had incomplete degrees and talked to them about "Wouldn't it be great if you could do this?" and "Do you think that you could stand up in the faculty meeting if I proposed this and speak to it?" Then I put together a work committee and included a bunch of the key faculty who had wives who had either professional degrees or incomplete degrees and let them be at the forefront of it. They worked off my document but ultimately they made it their own. And once they made it their own, they got it through.

None of these things sound like anything, except that at the time I did them they were brand new and they were facing enormous opposition. So if that's leadership, then it's partly working through other people, but it's partly speaking on behalf of other people in a way that makes people think for the moment, "Yes, I believe that. Yes, I identify with that. Yes, that's really my point of view."

Leadership as a process of working with people and through people is further illustrated by the statement that one Instigator offered about surrounding herself with "tremendously talented people. . . . I tend to get more credit sometimes than I deserve. I do deserve credit for hiring them and helping them to do a really bang-up job."

The ability to work with others rests on both interpersonal skills and self-awareness. Perhaps one of the most significant skills the Instigators modeled for the Inheritor generation involves their ability to integrate their capacities as strategists, facilitators, and communicators. In addition, these women are perceptive and they learn fast:

I can organize and manage, but after a couple of years, I found someone who liked what I have to call the administrative director part of what I had been doing. In other words, she kept the secretaries happy and the paper flowing and made sure that we had the files organized and the systems operating and all of those sorts of things. That's not me. . . . When I came here I didn't know what a foundation was, and I barely knew [from my family] what a corporation was except that it manufactured clothes with labels on it. So I've learned all that being here, but I have noticed what I prefer and what I don't. What I like very much about what we have now is that I have someone on the staff who's the development director. I don't mind at all going out and giving the pitch for the program I think is important and care about for the institution, but the day-by-day putting it together . . . When you're running an organization you have to make decisions and you can't do all that, because if you did it you wouldn't be running the organization. You need to find other people to do it. But I've only discovered that. When you get a Ph.D. in English, that's not what you learn. So I learned it all sort of doing this, and without having someone to teach me.

No less important than organizational expertise are the sensitivity to timing and the capacity to "let go" of efforts when necessary. These qualities suggest the sophisticated and subtle dimensions of exercising leadership. One Instigator observed that "I had spent three and a half years or so building good bridges and I was really in a very sturdy administrative position as I walked into the [women's] commission position, but the moment you really begin to put teeth into the commission I could just see that I was cutting off the avenues that I had earlier opened. . . . It seemed to me that one of the difficulties in affirmative action is sort of the dead-end route and the kinds of antagonisms that one develops in that arena. So, yes, I developed the plan. We got it going. I think it was a successful beginning, and I got out as fast as I could."

Despite their successes, some Instigators were uncomfortable with or even unwilling to accept the mantle "leader," which may suggest genuine humility and/or a commitment to collective action. Their discomfort might also represent the independence and sense of self that the Instigators brought to their tasks, as well as perhaps some natural resistance to labels. When we asked them to talk about themselves and how they see their leadership, they responded with reflections like these:

I just think I'm the one with the idea. I know what we're going to do, and it tends to be project-oriented leadership. The reason I see myself as a natural leader in certain respects, not all, is that I believe in collective action. It's not enough to have something clear to me. It's got to take place, and to take place it's got to be clear to other people. It's that simple. And so the craft or the art and the craft of leadership for me is making things clear to other people, not telling them what to do or how to do it or running their lives. So it's a very special notion of leadership. . . .

Everybody who knows my leadership style knows that I'm very nonauthoritarian and nondirective, and can tolerate ambiguity much longer than most other people. That's what people say. They call it my laid-back style, but more precisely defined, it's a willingness to tolerate no closure and ambiguity for a very long time in the expectation that the decision once made will be a better one for allowing all that stuff to surface. . . . I have a low tolerance for *meeting* decision making. Not that I don't believe in collective decision making. I'm very action oriented. That's a strength and a weakness . . . so maybe it's not leadership in the ordinary sense of having followers. . . . It's leadership in the sense of defining the topics that other people aren't able to yet see but could see if you do the initial mapping for them.

The sense of common enterprise, but also the excitement of being challenged, of not doing what is predictable, stimulated these observations by another Instigator:

One day I had this vision of the future, and the vision of the future was this sort of ladder to heaven, and one rung was an assistant professor of English, then you went to associate, then you went to full, then you went to emeritus, and then you died. What horrified me about that vision of that ladder was not being an English professor . . . what horrified me was that somehow you could see it all, you knew it all, you knew exactly what you were going to do and what it would take to go from A to B. And what I loved about what I did, this crazy thing of getting a Ph.D. in English and then working in an institute of politics was that I didn't know what was around the next corner. . . . We make decisions as we're going along because the world out there is shifting, women's position in politics is changing and we'll watch that. So in a way, I sit here running an organization but I see myself as a scholar of the subject, though I don't do scholarship in the traditional ways of writing refereed articles for academic journals now. . . . I have a hard time with people who come here . . . and use the pronoun "you all" to describe what's happening, instead of "we" . . . who don't identify with the operation and who don't work out a sense of contributing to and building the respectability, the credibility, the good name for good work, of this center.

Another instigator described the collective effort and her orchestration of it by comparing it to a theater performance: "When you're directing a play, first of all your work is extremely visible and you are completely dependent on other people to carry it out. At some point you have to let them alone and let the show go on. You cannot direct in front of the audience. You have to let it go and trust the people to not only follow your general conception, but even to improvise on it and to make it even better and to add their own creative skills to it. And I think those kinds of ideas have formed my leadership style, if you want to call it that."

As our leaders noted, choices and preferences about style demand some critical self-analysis as well as analysis of their effects: "I think I am a good leader by administering what I believe. In that sense of leadership, the low profile has helped, because I stand for things, I've always stood for things that were unpopular. I've had an exciting and satisfying life along with a lot of problems, just like every other human being you ever meet. Any leadership, it seems to me, is partly being willing to appear to be bigger than life, even though you know that you're just a little person in spite of the amplifier and magnifying glass that's put on you." In the words of another leader, "My own orientation has never gone very far from being a scientist, and I'm very uncomfortable constructing political arguments that don't have a good sound basis in fact. I think people trust what I say. They know I don't shoot off my mouth without a reason. . . . It depends on how excited I am about the problem at that moment." A third leader's analysis was that "I can be abrasive at times, and I have had to be over the years, and there have been stages in our development when I've been very tough—but basically, my style is collaborative and to try to pull people in, and I've grown even more sophisticated at it over the years because I'm more sensitive to what's causing the problem. I certainly in the early years didn't understand as much about human nature as I do now, so when I meet impediments now I am more able to work it in a calmer and supportive style to help people come around to something that I need to do." And another leader concluded that "So in that sense I think that if what you want to be is an activist probably an emphasis on the goal rather than the means makes you a stronger leader because that's how big leaders get there. But that's not me. Intellectually also, I don't want to read cards. So you can say that I do neither of these things well but I think I'm kind of an interesting mixture, and what I am good at is mixing those, being a bridge. And so for better or for worse that's where I have ended up, in the middle of a lot of different things. Playing the kind of interpretive role which, as I say, means in some sense that you're not really of any one of these groups, but you are somewhere in between."

Effective leadership demands the ability to assess a situation, to engage others in a collective effort, and to bring about needed change. The women Instigators suggested that they have been politically adept, willing to take risks, and perceptive—particularly in the sense of being attuned to their environments. Above all, they emphasized the critical use of outstanding interpersonal and communication skills.

Positional Leadership

Past studies of leadership have focused mainly on positional leaders. These studies describe the characteristics and attributes of leaders, the leaders' effects on followers, and the tasks of leadership. Our study also examines positional leadership—particularly leadership provided by women college and university presidents. By focusing on *women* positional leaders we hope to expand our understanding of the concept of leadership and also provide some new and different perspectives about leaders and leadership.

In the first chapter we offered a feminist conceptual model of leadership. That model rests on the assumption that leadership manifests itself when there is an action to bring about change in an organization, an institution, or the social system—in other words, an action to make a positive difference in people's lives. Leadership, then, is conceived as a creative process that results in change. The leader, by virtue of her position, permits and enables others to accomplish the desired change through collective effort. Thus, in our study we focus a great deal of attention on the process of empowerment. How and by what means does the leader empower others? How does she delegate responsibility? What support or rewards does she provide? How do networks form?

During the interviews, we asked the positional leaders and other participants in our investigation to describe what is involved in accomplishing change. We also asked them to describe how they go about empowering others and mobilizing the collective action toward the desired change. We asked them to tell us about the strategies they use.

Power and *influence* are terms often used in studies of leaders and leadership. Consequently, we asked: Do the women in our study view themselves as powerful agents? Do they feel that they have personal power? Or do they view themselves as influential but not necessarily as powerful? We asked them to tell us about their self-perceptions in general and to rate themselves on a number of personal attributes or traits.

The Dynamics of Change. According to the women positional leaders, change occurs when you first see the problem, get a clear picture of it, and then mobilize others by organizing the collective effort to bring about desired change within the existing structure, not necessarily by overthrowing what is there but by working within it. Based on her personal experience as a positional leader and her response to the needs she has faced, one of the women in the sample said about the process of change: "I see the problem and then I form the organization to solve it, and I am very quick to determine the solution and then work very hard, like forever, to solve it and to keep changing that solution as time [goes on]." She emphasized that one has to be flexible and make adjustments within the system: "You have to keep making changes that hopefully do not ever tamper with the basic integrity of what you are trying to do. But one has to make . . . adjustments so that the system accepts this [change you are trying to make]. Something has to be done to negotiate out the differences, and then you can move . . . [and] make a little more progress." Thus, she sees the problem, conceptualizes its solution, and then makes changes within the existing social structure.

However, change is not brought about single-handedly; you need to develop a network of like-minded people and to evolve a collective effort. Earlier in this chapter we called attention to the skills of the Instigators in orchestrating group efforts. According to positional leaders in the sample: "to change things at the university it required that faculty and students be united—it was not a splinter group, if it was they would have been ignored"; "the way to make a decision and make it stick is to listen to all constituents"; "change occurs by hard work, by inspiring people to form a vision, by networking and having people come together to accomplish change."

Change, as we witness it through these women leaders, takes place within the existing system. They challenged the system, but they also recognized and understood the existing values and structure. As part of this, the strength of having a network, an infrastructure, cannot be overlooked: "We just linked together. We met periodically; there was an organization called 'The Women's Network' which was a huge organization, but it really started with a dinner. . . . We figured out one day that we could actually work a major policy issue through the administration without [it] ever touching a man's hand until it got to the president's desk. That is how well placed the women were." This description refers to the women's network during the Carter administration. It was a network of women placed in important public policy positions or government agencies who had recognized the importance of collective energy to move the system.

Gerda Lerner (1984, p. 36) has described this feminist process of change aptly: first there is an awareness of a wrong, then a sense of sisterhood develops, followed by the autonomous definition of goals and strategies for change, and finally, an alternative vision for the future emerges. This progression is often bound up with an increasing sense of feminist empowerment.

Strategies for Empowerment. To further identify leadership strategies and style, we asked the positional leaders in our sample the following questions:

- In terms of leadership, how would you describe yourself? What characteristics have you brought to your work which enable you or others to view you as a leader?
- In bringing about change, what leadership style or strategies have you relied on?
- From your perspective, what are the essential ingredients of leadership?
- Do you think of yourself as someone who has or has had power?

Their responses to these questions centered around three general themes: clarity of values, listening to and empowering others, and doing your homework.

Clarity of values was especially important. As we have emphasized earlier in this book, the role of values in the leadership of these women was articulated in terms of the vision guiding their behavior. The positional leaders also saw their primary role as one of providing vision—having a point of view that clearly articulates an institutional mission. Trust and integrity were words often used by them. Building trust, trusting others, maintaining your integrity—"if you do, you never get trapped"—commitment to women and people of color (the commitment to human rights and justice underscored previously) were strong, commonly held values: "I will work hard for equal salaries here. I will go after any element that I think is discriminatory, and there was a lot of it here when I arrived." "One of the commitments I've got here is that no kid should get out of this college without a real commitment to being a volunteer." "What I feel passionate about is helping women and minorities."

This caring, value-oriented commitment as the centerpiece of leadership, a theme often heard from Instigators, comes across strongly again in the statement made by one of our positional leaders: "You know, I think [the reason for my leadership activities] was because I cared passionately about the concept of rights for women. In fact, sometimes people ask me about leadership and the first thing I ever say is, 'You've got to care desperately about something.'" It is not enough to have a vision, however; leadership requires sharing that vision, empowering others, and creating a collective that acts to bring about the desired change.

A second important theme in our respondents' comments was that of *listening to and empowering others.* In hierarchical paradigms of leadership that rest on the leader-follower model, the positional leader is someone who has authority and who controls information and resources in order to accomplish particular objectives. In other words, this person exercises power over others as she or he "leads." In contrast, our respondents viewed power as a relational process: "We had power jointly as a group." According to them, hierarchical power is problematic in that it can create an attitude of worship by the followers that, in turn, imposes great expectations of what a leader can and should be able to accomplish. It can intimidate those around you and thus stifle creativity. They affirmed not a need for power in the form of control but rather power in the form of empowerment. This is why, for example, every one of the women college and university presidents talked about having "influence" rather than power. Influence was preferred because it was seen in interpersonal and in value-oriented terms. They recognized that by virtue of their position—being the president of an institution—they had authority and that others attribute power to them (in essence, positional authority creates symbolic power). However, they used their position as a power base to influence and to develop networks that, in turn, became the powerful agents of change. By empowering others, they were able to create a collective that worked synergistically (synergy is, indeed, collective power-energy that is the result of combining efforts).

What is refreshing in responses like this is the openness of these leaders' style. They appear to be nondefensive and to value their co-workers. If you value others, you listen to them, you trust them, and you are receptive to their pointing out your mistakes or other problems. Recognizing that leadership requires collective action, you choose your co-workers to complement your talents, you reward them, and you give them feedback. These points are summed up in the following list of empowering behaviors favored by our interviewees:

1. You meet people on their own turf and you listen.
2. You hire strong people who complement you; you are not defensive; you let them point out problems and mistakes.
3. You make them feel good; you give them feedback; you make them visible; you give others the credit they deserve.
4. You value collegiality; thus you consult with others a lot and you work through consensus.

One respondent provided this example of "meeting people on their own turf": "I brown-bag lunch with each department. I always tell them, 'This is your hour. What you want to brag about or complain about, or be sure that I know about.'" "I listen and try to build bridges of communication." "I do listen hard and I think I learn from what I hear and I do not come in with a lot of preconceived notions about what we ought to do."

Having strong people or people that complement you is not a threatening issue. These leaders are confident and they know themselves well enough that they appreciate other people's strengths. They are not competitive, they are cooperative: "I think that the most important thing is to recognize what you are good at and what you are not and be sure that you hire people around you who will fill in the gaps." "There are also an awful lot of things that you do that are full of holes and [it's important to have] some people around you who will tell you that there are problems and who will help you sort through them and won't try to mask the problems." "I like strong people and if I possibly can I will surround myself with the most talented, the most outspoken, and the strongest people I can." "I always hire people that are varied. . . . I'm not afraid of hiring people who are better than I am or of giving them visibility." "I like to work with very strong people. I enjoy that. I don't find that any threat." "I believe so strongly in delegation and I believe so strongly in letting people move it along as far as they can, I am a delegator and a supporter."

These leaders give praise and credit where they are due; they provide feedback and they reward their co-workers appropriately: "If someone in this room is a member of a junior or senior staff and has made a suggestion that was a good one, they would be publicly praised for it. I would not take it away from them. It would be theirs and they would get the praise." "Your job is to get them to do their best. . . . You have got to make them feel good in order to get them to be effective."

Most important is that they believe in the collaborative, collegial style of leadership and in the importance of reaching consensus: "The style of a college community, a university setting is a negotiation style. It's a collaborative style. It's a collegial style." "Keep your people informed about what you are doing and what you are thinking and constantly ask for their views and opinions." "I like very much to work with people and accomplish things with people through people." "I really consult quite a lot." "I've tried to encourage grass roots [activities]. . . . I'd rather have a good bit of support for the issues we're addressing." "I am a process person. I do value the Quaker tradition of this place and how decisions are made." They empower by enabling others to do their best: "One of the things I find is very important to do is to get people, whether staff or faculty, to do things they have no idea they can do." "I am interested in enabling very good people to do their work with great freedom."

Another theme emphasized by our respondents is the need to *do your homework*. The importance of being prepared, knowing what you are talking about, doing your research, planning a lot, and developing a blueprint was mentioned by all of our women leaders when asked to talk about the leadership process they engaged in. Having a vision and being a good listener have to be coupled with the need to be prepared by having done your homework. One wonders how much of this is a gender-related trait and approach, a consequence of the notion that being female in an important position requires you to be twice as good as any male in a similar role or position: "I tried to always do my homework. [I] never went to a meeting unprepared. I tried to find out what other people thought so I would be comfortable in the discussion." "[I am] very task oriented and [I've tried] to be as good as I can possibly be at it, very conscientious and working long hours." "Building trust [must be accomplished by] knowing your stuff."

These women know how to use resources and they do. They use internal and external resources to gain perspective and information. One of the college presidents, when she accepted the position of president, "did research like a scholar would do." She went to the library and talked to other administrators. She wanted to learn as much as she could about the task. There is a seriousness with which these women approach their task of leadership. They are learners, students about themselves, the institution, and the process of leadership.

Empowerment Through Scholarship and Teaching

As noted earlier, we see feminist scholarship as a form of leadership, since it emerged to produce social change that would benefit women and other groups: "I do think of myself as an intellectual and probably one of the best in the country. I also think that the way it manifests itself is to serve as a catalyst for other people's development." "I see my role with the graduate students as simply teaching them everything, both politically and academically, and empowering them." Thus we chose to study the leadership of fifteen highly visible scholars whose work focused on women, whether women's history, the psychology of women, women and education, or women's role in the workplace and the economy. Because of who they are and because of their passion for knowledge and understanding and for telling women's story, many of these scholars have also served in positional capacities, as active participants in organizations and institutions. They have been chairs of state commissions on the status of women, members of important councils and task forces, trustees of colleges, and presidents of their disciplinary organizations. Two of them have served in important presidential appointments: one as a member of the cabinet and the second as director of a major federal agency.

While their scholarship ultimately plays a role in transforming the disciplines and the institutions in which they teach, their leadership is also manifest in teaching and mentoring students and junior faculty. Through their gift of teaching and their commitment to mentoring, they empower and coach the next generation of scholars and agents of social change. They communicate ideas clearly and persuasively: "If I opened my mouth and started talking I could get people to listen. I could persuade people." "Teaching gave me a lot of confidence and gave me the sense that I could speak my mind in public and people would listen. . . . [It was] an enormous affirmation. . . . Lecturing gave me another platform, and so the kind of lecturing I did was quite partisan. . . . It was scholarly, but it was partisan." "I think the debating team was very empowering because I learned to speak extemporaneously. . . . I am a good public speaker. I am a good teacher. I am always fairly quick in making myself felt. . . . I am articulate and have a lot of facility with words."

Teaching is essential to the identity of these women and how they go about making a difference by transforming individuals and institutions:

> I consider teaching an absolutely integral part of my intellectual and professional development. I'm a very dedicated teacher and I'm proud of my teaching. . . . I think that the medium by which an intellectual mediates between her theoretical work and her active engagement in the society is teaching. To me, teaching has always been the place in which I could translate what I have learned to other people and inspire them to in turn translate it into something else. . . . I just feel very strongly about teaching as an obligation of the scholar. . . . I feel that as a teacher I am out to change lives. That's my goal. I'm out to have an impact on that student, to change that student's attitude toward himself or herself, to inspire that student to do better and to go on and do differently. I have been able to do that. I think probably that next to my family, the most important human relations that I have are with my students. That's a very important part of my life and career.

Our respondents see teaching not only as a responsibility but as a very rewarding experience in itself: "I really love to teach and I love supervising dissertations. . . . I would always want to keep some

element of teaching in what I was doing. . . . It is personally
rewarding."

Mentoring of their students and junior colleagues represents
leadership through the process of empowerment: "I think I am
much more deliberate in my efforts to work closely with a select
group of students, most of whom are women. That's one-on-one,
and it takes enormous amounts of time and also is enormously
rewarding. . . . I usually have a graduate assistant. . . . I don't play
the game as some have tried to play it, which is [to] predict the
future for them or place them in the future. . . . My role is to help
them discover who they are and give them some gifts for their jour-
ney." The scholars want to influence younger women, and they
believe that by training the next generation of Ph.D.'s they will be
training the Inheritors of the legacy they have created:

> I am involved with about twenty Harvard graduate women
> students in an endeavor that brought a group of women to-
> gether, not for consciousness raising and not for political ac-
> tion, but to address the issues set out in the *Handbook of
> Adolescent Psychology*. . . . The adolescent girls had not been
> studied. . . . We had meetings at my house. All of us met once
> a month. . . . I am so aligned with the part of feminism that
> wants to use women's experience as a basis for reconsidering
> existing institutions and structures and assumptions. . . . I
> wanted to make changes and I noticed . . . that if you train a
> group of Ph.D.'s you can make change. This is what I believe,
> and part of my effort within this small domain that I work in
> is to try to empower more women to work in that way. I would
> like to influence the next generation of developmental
> psychologists.

Senior faculty members are mentors not only to students but to
junior faculty as well: "I take very seriously the mentoring role with
junior faculty so that I am instantly called for advice. . . . It's a role
that I really see . . . [as] my debt to the women's movement. I'm in
the position I am in because of the women's movement. My sense
is that the role of—[people] like me—is to keep the door open, and
the way one does that is not only by fighting but by creating op-

portunities and by personally mentoring and offering the kind of political advice that I got or did not get from others." Thus, these scholars believe in the power of transforming individuals as the way of transforming institutions and, ultimately, society. They have been able to transform individuals by mentoring them directly and by providing the knowledge and information that becomes the vehicle for raising consciousness: "I believe that women's history is the best consciousness raiser there is. And it's the only consciousness raiser we can use that appeals to all kinds of women, regardless of their politics, class, or social standing. . . . So to me, the best spreading of the best of women's history to the women's movement, and through the women's movement, to broader and broader sectors of the population, and especially to young women and men as they are growing up, I think that's the tool for change." For these women, the ongoing dialogue and observation that are part of the experience of empowering others is a vital part of their own self-development as well: "It has been through interchanges between the scholarly and activist worlds, as well as in keeping an eye on what has been happening to women's position, that I think my work and I have developed."

Self-Assessment of Personal Qualities

While the major focus of this chapter has been on style and strategies of leadership we felt that some attention to personal attributes could be helpful in a study of leadership. Thus we asked the question, what are the personal qualities that guide these women in their quest for social change? This question drew us to the frequent focus of leadership studies—leader attributes. The notion of leaders as special people prompts us to want to identify the unique qualities that characterize them. This search, especially in our modern, complex society, is often motivated by a need for information that can be used for training purposes. While there are no traits that will guarantee successful leadership in all situations, certain general attributes appear repeatedly—for example, physical vitality and energy, intelligence, courage, confidence, and flexibility.

From our study, some similar qualities emerged. Our initial view of the Instigators evolved from their accomplishments: what they contributed to the lives of women in a rapidly changing period of social history. In their interviews they repeatedly stressed the passion and vision they brought to the challenges they accepted. A closer look into the elements of their leadership, using their own words and reports, confirmed many shared qualities and experiences:

- High activity and energy levels
- Appetites for challenge, problem solving, and risk taking
- Obstacles and personal setbacks to accept and overcome
- Intellectual competence and the underpinnings of strong academic backgrounds
- Personal awareness and confidence, continuously honed by wide exposure to life experiences—work, community service, cultural diversity
- Support for their commitment from family or friends or models and mentors

The women positional leaders in the study attributed similar qualities to themselves: physical stamina, intelligence, assertiveness, and determination.

Our respondents' general intelligence was reflected in statements such as:

> "I have a good memory."
> "I know when something doesn't add up."
> "I am very good at writing and speaking."
> "I have a quick mind."
> "I am articulate."
> "I have an exceptional attention span."

They describe themselves too as being high-energy people and in very good health. Invariably, they talk about how little sleep they need and report that they can work very hard for long periods of time. They also describe themselves as assertive and decisive:

> "I am strong."
> "I am decisive."

"I act."

"I speak my mind."

"I am willing to take risks."

"I make tough decisions."

"I am independent."

"I have an 'I can do anything' attitude."

"Energy," "loyalty," and "commitment" got the highest ratings as personal traits they consider very characteristic of themselves. High endorsement was also given to traits such as: "intuitiveness," "resourcefulness," "self-confidence," and "adaptability."

Looking at these leaders' self-descriptions, one is impressed with their high level of self-esteem. They acknowledge liking themselves and being self-accepting. They are not modest about their intellectual abilities. They can say "I am unusually bright" with a great deal of comfort. Even when things do not work, they do not see themselves as complainers. They appear to move with resilience. Their self-confidence, passion, and sense of having a mission in life—to make a difference in this world—may be what enable them to persist with such resilience and to accomplish so much. These women are strong, self-reliant, committed, and caring.

The scholars' self-descriptions echo the same qualities: "intelligence," "perseverance," "resourcefulness," "leadership," and "curiosity." It is not surprising that as scholars and researchers they endorse traits that are essential to their becoming successful. Curiosity is what drives them to uncover the truth about knowledge, and resourcefulness and perseverance are the traits that have enabled them to overcome prejudice and discrimination to emerge successfully as the leaders of feminist scholarship and social activism.

Instigators, positional leaders, and scholars expressed in quite personal terms what they did as leaders. Their approaches vary with respect to individual perspectives and emphases, but their skills, strategies, and personal attributes began to sound amazingly unified. They view leadership as the challenge and the opportunity to work with others, and their words echo again and again the genuine belief that collective effort and the empowerment of others provide the critical elements for significant social change.

CHAPTER 7

Strains and Costs of Leadership

> I think it's important if you don't have to spend your
> time and energy being lonely and fighting that . . .
> and to have the support of someone who believes in
> you, who says "yes, you can do it" and "yes, that's
> wonderful and I'm proud of you."
>
> —*Instigator*

Leaders seldom escape the challenges, obstacles, or pains that test other human beings. For example, illnesses and deaths struck family members and some cherished colleagues of the women in our study. Several women were divorced. Some lost jobs or missed significant opportunities because of discrimination. And all encountered numerous hurdles in their pursuit of social change. But more often than not they found ways of coping with these challenges and of renewing themselves.

Obstacles

Several of the women related the strains of literally living "in the shadows" of their husbands and the frequent conflict that brought them. One leader recalled an occasion when she and her husband were entertained by a professional woman who in her own way wanted to help women and was very supportive in the beginning. . . . We were invited over to her house for dinner. I was invited with [my husband]—he was the new faculty member. . . . We got there and we had dinner downstairs, and after dinner we were sitting and talking. I was in this long discussion about Ibsen's plays with a male member of the faculty when the dean herself—she was in the leadership role and she had these new faculty people in, twenty people or thirty people there, for that buffet supper— she came to me and tapped me on the shoulder in the middle of this conversation and asked me if I would like to join her and the women upstairs. It was like a nineteenth-century novel. I mean I was in a rage. I went upstairs with her and I found all the women, some of whom were wives and there in their role only as wives, but there were other faculty types as I recall, or women like myself with professional lives, and we were up there while the men had cigars downstairs. [My husband] couldn't believe it. I couldn't believe it. I still can't believe that she did it, and this was the early 1970s.

Others faced nepotism rules or a general atmosphere of gender discrimination. In the words of one Instigator: "I had never meant to be an administrator, I had meant to be a doctor, and then I shifted my sights and said, okay, I will be a college teacher and scholar. And by the time I finished my degree, I had gotten a lot of praise and important people were saying everything I wrote was publishable, and what a career I had, only to discover in the fifties that I couldn't get a teaching job." Another woman related this episode:

[I arrived] at [institution], looking for a job as the appendage to a male and found myself handed down to the personnel assistant officer to be given a typing test. I was thirty-three, I had all but a dissertation. I had four years of experience in New York. I'd been near the top of my class—that did not matter at all, not only because I was a female, but because I was doing what females did, namely, I was following a man somewhere. . . . And I was only semiconscious of what was going on until I was handed this typing test and shorthand test. The typing test I could pass with "women" colors. I was good at typing. But the shorthand test I had to fake and so I was under a certain amount of tension and anxiety about the shorthand test. The woman giving me the shorthand test looked across the table at me and there was a moment of mutual commiseration. It wasn't her fault. We were both part of a system beyond our control. And I think I saw the systemic nature of my problem, not only that it was a personal problem, that it was a fault of my personal decision to follow a man, but there was something bigger at work.

Even more personal were the reflections of one of the women who experienced the breakup of a marriage in the decade we describe:

I come from being a fifties housewife; although I had done other things, I really became much more of an individual and a person within the marriage. I also became successful rather rapidly, and although my husband was very supportive, and very pleased with what I was doing, he was very pleased as long as he was giving me advice. In a quaint way I began to know as much and maybe more than he did about what needed to be done. I am a fast learner and learned the politics and the strategies. That was when things began to fall apart, because he was giving me advice and I wouldn't take it.

Previously, anything that he said, I was "oh, that's wonderful, dear. Yes." So I became much more of an individual and began to make demands on him. I made a lot of demands very rapidly—and he could not accommodate them that rapidly, in terms of equality within the marriage, and so the marriage broke up. It might have broken up anyway; it didn't break up over women's issues as such. It broke up over my seeing myself as a person, working full time, for the first time—working very hard and having to do a second job of housework and car pools and shopping and children and all of that, and balking at that, not because of the women's ideology as such. It was just hard to do all of that and I felt it was only fair that he help. And we really broke up around those kinds of issues.

These women faced unique challenges because they blazed new pathways, creating structures for new ideas, working outside traditions and outside of the academic and professional mainstream. In trying to build a new organization, one leader admitted, "I was really very inexperienced. . . . In fact, I didn't know how to mobilize the resources that might be around. It took me a long time to learn some of those things because I was alone a lot and not interacting with the other people doing the same thing." Others spoke of the frustrations of establishing institutional relationships for themselves and their services to women, especially in the 1960s social context that was dominated by campus unrest and a changing cast of administrators. They were also faced with the additional burden of having to raise money for the new organizations or programs—something that often resulted in rejection. But they usually responded with resilience: "I didn't know what they needed, there were a lot of needs analyses, so to speak, that had to be done and getting to the right person, and to be sometimes laughed at and told we don't need this or to be asked who is this organization? It was constant rejection, and some support. So I know that one of the things of my life is I can live with rejection. This is a critical component I think, in any kind of major accomplishment, to be able to take that rejection and not see it as a personal rejection and something that's ever going to stop you." "It meant going back to [the companies] year after year making the case, being rejected, and going back still with a positive sense of what could be accomplished . . . coming into every year barely balancing my budget—a cliffhanger. . . . In the things I've done, it's taken such a terrifically high level of motivation. You have to take so much guff. You have to take so many rejections. You're swimming so much upstream."

The purpose of our study was to highlight accomplishments and to explore aspects of leadership development. Neither we nor the women leaders dwelt on the inevitable costs, but the trade-offs of leadership deserve some reiteration. As one woman remarked, "You also pay . . . in terms of your physical self. . . . I don't know now if I could do that again, to work as hard as I feel I worked during that time. . . . I don't know if it's that I am older, so I have that excuse, or if it's psychological, but I don't want to do that again."

Time spent and energy expended clearly exceeded normal limits for these women, though this could be a mixed blessing. Some noted their unusual vitality: "I have energy all over the place . . . good health and a lot of energy." Another boasted, "I can sleep on command and eat on command and I'm cautious; I don't have any habits that are debilitating," but she also acknowledged that "you get exhausted." Another mentioned constant time constraints: "My time is structured. I use it all. I use even all of my leisure time very actively." And a third observed that "the cost is you have to really be ready to work your tail off for a long, long time. It's very draining in terms of the kind of hours that you have to spend." But as one said, "If I were a man that would be considered having a wonderful, high energy level. I've been described as a workaholic. I've been described as driven, and in a way that tickles me. If I am, then I was at birth."

These themes and voices were repeated over and over again. The universal frustration is "not enough time." Lack of time interferes with their personal needs—needs to nurture themselves, to spend time on reading and writing, or to be with friends. Time is very precious to them and they have very little personal time: "All your social time is taken up, and what seems like social time is work." "I think what gets to you really is that you don't have any time. . . . You do work seven days a week, pretty much from five o'clock in the morning to eleven o'clock at night." "It is very draining in terms of the kind of hours that you have to spend."

These leaders report being frustrated by their lack of control over their schedule or by being scheduled for the institution five out of seven nights a week: "There are some days when I look at my schedule and wonder 'How in the hell did I ever get myself into this?' . . . I can never do anything in depth anymore. It's hard to sit down and write anything. And if you're trained to be a scholar, and if you really like writing and reading the way that I do, you don't get to do that kind of stuff. It's very frustrating."

While not enough time is a universal complaint, women who never married also talk about the costs and frustration(s) of singlehood and its effects on someone who is in a very public role. These costs take many forms: not having someone close to you with whom you can share your frustrations and from whom you can get support, experiencing the sometimes undesirable expectations others have of you, or feeling unprotected from the sexist assumption that you can be available to any man at any time.

These problems are vividly portrayed in their words: "The first couple of years were rough. First the student body wanted a father figure. I didn't have a husband. I had some credibility problems with the student body." "For a single woman, I think there is more demand on your time because they don't think they're intruding on anything."

Other sacrifices were cited. One woman observed, for example, that she had tended to give up leisure and vacations, and what she thought of as "sports," eventually realizing that "I had never been on a horse . . . been in a canoe . . . near a ski slope." Despite the presence of colleagues and the women's network, other leaders talked about the loss of time for deeper friends: "I often recognize I move too fast, that I don't do the things that would really build continuing deep relationships. I meet so many people. I get along with too many people. I don't mean that in the negative sense. There are just too many people in my life for me to be able to do that with any more than I already have. I have a close family. . . . I don't mean that I don't have friends, but deep relationships I would say. And I think that's one of the big costs that I feel. . . . I just don't have the time or energy. It isn't that I don't wishfully think about this, but I haven't written my 'thank you letters' yet to the people whose houses I stayed in three weeks ago. It's that kind of thing that really doesn't endear you to other people."

Sometimes questions about costs brought back vivid memories: "I got to a point where I felt I had the burdens of most of society on my shoulders. We used to joke about it. We figured about 70 percent of the population were our constituents and we kept telling people we were not the minority, we're clearly the majority. . . . There's never eight hours a day. It's ten to twelve. At the same time, during a part of those years, a lot of my extracurricular activities were involved in women's organizations and women's problems, and my life was completely consumed by that, and I got to a point . . . where I couldn't go to a cocktail party or a dinner party without getting into an argument because you either got asked what you did for a living or there would always be some guy who would make some smart-ass remark." Or, such questions elicited statements about current demands: "I think at this juncture, my real problem is how to have time enough to smell the flowers. I think that is a part of my life and you use up your intellectual capital. As you look back at my career pattern, I haven't had much time to build my capital."

Responding to whether they ever felt lonely as leaders, some felt loneliness was intrinsic to the role: "I think it's very lonely. I think the higher you go, the less you are able to admit that this has you baffled, that you don't really have a good answer for it, or you don't even feel competent and qualified to take that on. It certainly happened to me many times and I was unwilling to admit it, not to myself—I think I always knew—but to other people because that's a world of high leadership which lots of other people would like to be in. . . . It's highly competitive." Others had a different reaction: "No. I've never felt lonely in the leadership role because there are so many more women around me—because of the support system. That's really what the support systems did, was to take away that loneliness." "No. I experience a lot of pleasure that I impose on myself because I want very much not only for [organization] to continue to exist while it's needed but for it to really do a good job."

Replenishment

While the women leaders admitted to drains and pressures on their personal lives, they also underscored the self-correcting mechanisms they have adopted to balance life demands, to renew energies, to "build . . . capital." Renewal involves familiar activities—art, music, and frequently out-of-doors experiences such as walking, running, and swimming. For many, physical exercise is crucial. One woman described its multiple effects: "I exercise a lot and that has something to do with looking younger than my age, and that is a way to let off some of the steam. I've used exercise to do that."

Many, indeed, find replenishment from physical activity: mountain climbing, tennis, walking, and exercising. "From the days in college, I've mountain climbed. I book for two weeks every summer . . . in the Canadian Rockies where I hike." "The last two summers I've taken a full month off. One of my closest friends talked me into taking a month off and we went off to the Himalayas."

Another woman stated: "Yes, I like to read, but I think my biggest rejuvenator is doing some physical exercise. I just went to tennis camp this summer." "I walked across England last summer. That's what I did, and that's what I like to do. It is something very different, very active. I walked 109 miles in twelve days. And that was wonderfully refreshing for me. I walk for an hour every morning between 6:00 and 7:00."

Many of the women leaders' responses reinforce their images as academics and social activists, often buoyed by the work itself, by the new challenges they continue to seek, or by the balance they have learned—or are learning—to put into their own lives. One woman admitted, "I want to be the first kid on the block, to keep coming up with new issues so that I don't get bored." She said, "I never found what I was doing hard. I found it tremendously challenging and exciting. I have been waiting to be burned out. . . . I go through cycles every now and then, where I just feel overwhelmed and I've got too many things to do. So I've learned over the years to say no, but it's very hard to turn down things that are interesting. I've learned how to turn down things I don't want to do."

As suggested earlier, some find replenishment and needed balance in family relationships. One woman shared her reality:

When my father had his store and had to stay open until 11:00 at night and he wasn't making much of a living, his choice was that he didn't go to whatever I was doing at school including my junior high school graduation. . . . I know this had a tremendous impact on me because there was virtually nothing that would have kept me from going to something that my daughter was doing that I thought was important for her to have a parent there. And I never ever resented it. She put fewer demands on me than I put on myself. I knew very clearly that

I was choosing it for me because I needed to be there and wanted to be there myself.

So what I'm saying is for all the years she was growing up, my private life, which was in those years largely my life as a single parent, was terribly, terribly important to me. I didn't need much else. I was happy to do my job seven days a week and whatever I needed to do, but not if I felt that in any way it deprived [my daughter] of what I thought was important for her to have. . . . What I'm telling you about are my own personal priorities. And maybe some of that came out of a reaction to what I felt my father didn't do or couldn't do. . . . It must have come out of a need that I have. When you say, what's the personal price? I could throw myself into a job seven days a week, twenty-four hours a day, and totally let that take over. I know I could in the sense of doing it, and probably be pretty happy if it were imposed on me. But the choices I see myself making when that's not imposed . . . are always choices that involve some private life with somebody that has nothing to do with this work.

Another woman explained that her replenishment comes both from her family and from time spent alone:

My replenishment comes from my family involvement. My husband and my children mean a great deal to me and I enjoy them immensely. Without that, I'm not sure that my life would be quite as full and rich as it is. I know that there are women who feel that marriage and children are distracting, and they are, but it's a distraction I welcome. I've always felt that way—even as a graduate student; I had my babies when I was a graduate student. It meant a great deal to me even then to have some contact with what I felt was real and earthy: children and changing diapers and that kind of thing that ties you to real human needs of people. So family has always meant that to me and that means a couple or so books I haven't written and several essays and what have you that would have gotten done had I not been married or had children. But I think the trade-off is absolutely worth it.

I came to realize the other way in which I got replenishment was in traveling, that it allowed me to get away, to be by myself. I did a lot of thinking, did some reading. It took energy. It takes a lot out of you to get on a plane and fly to wherever for two or three days and come back. But I went East often and that five/six hour trip across the country was very good. I reflected on a lot of things, put things in perspective for myself. The more I think about it the more I think that that played a very major role in terms of replenishing my spirits. And, of course, once arriving at wherever I went and participating in conferences and meetings and whatever. I got replenished with new ideas, meeting people, sharing my own concerns and getting some feedback from people, and that meant a lot to me.

Partners play a very important supportive role. "My balance is my husband. . . . There is one strong influence in my life and that's him. He's a very unusual man. . . . I couldn't do anything without him." "I have a number of people that I talk to about a variety of different things, particularly my closest associates up here . . . and I talk to my husband. He's wonderful . . . wonderful. It's not that he demands being talked to, it's not that he tells you what to do and so on, but he hears."

Support sometimes comes from having help at home such as a housekeeper or from having a car and a driver. On the personal level, support comes from friends or a primary relationship. "Friends [replenish me] and I am very dependent on them because it's the only time I can turn off."

Besides friends the support may come from their administrative staff and the board of trustees: "I have a splendid administrative group. We're very close. . . . I think we're very compatible . . . and [I have an] absolutely first-rate board of trustees . . . I have a very supportive board chairman. . . . There are a lot of people I can turn to." "I go to [my chair of the board] and my friends. I will probably still go to him when he's not the chairman. . . . He is very loving. There's no one else on the board of trustees that I have anything like that relationship with."

For many the feeling that they have been engaged in a creative process, that they have been building a body of knowledge, as the case with the academic scholars, and that they are mentoring the next generation of scholars is, in itself, energizing and sustaining to them. "In some ways, all of the time that it costs has been more than repaid. I find a lot of this work enormously fulfilling. The sense of having built something creative is just wonderful."

The comments about their work attitudes, commitments, and satisfaction often overrode the demands they cited as inherent in their work: "The satisfaction was in seeing something get done. I think that I have always had to deal with two things: on the one hand, the ability to take the knocks—and I think I've had as many as anybody in our profession—and on the other hand, the recognition that the pleasure was in the doing. I really do understand about the sand castle mentality. It's taken me a long time but [I really understand and experience that] the pleasure is in the doing; when you go away the next day it's all gone and people don't even remember."

Friendships alluded to briefly have also been sustaining and empowering. "Once the women's movement started, we began to build up a network of friendships that has been incredibly strengthening and sustaining. And I could say today that in the history profession, I am a personal friend of maybe 150 of the best women historians in the country and of outstanding women in other intellectual fields in women's studies. I have personal experiences with them. I would call on them if I were in need. They would call on me. I would visit them. We see each other regularly. It's a network. It's a real sisterhood, and that has been incredibly important."

The network and friendships with other women form their support system. It is the *collective*. But the agenda is not finished, there is still plenty to be done. One scholar conveyed the sense many of the other women had that life, with all its challenges, is to be lived fully. "My activism takes the form of pounding away on my typewriter. I have many miles before I sleep, so much to learn and share and so much encouragement to dispense."

CHAPTER 8

Learning from the Past and Looking Toward the Future

> We have to create an alternate vision of personal re-
> lations of nurturance and we have to address the ques-
> tion in a nonpatriarchal society [of] who takes care of
> the children, the aged, and the nonperfect. That is the
> agenda.
>
> —*Instigator*

The women leaders in this study contributed the form and force of what we now talk about as the second wave of the women's movement. In truly landmark events and initiatives, they created new vehicles for studying women, teaching about women, and teaching women. They developed and produced major legislative changes to combat discrimination and to ennoble educational pur-poses and institutional commitments. They have been leaders who generated a climate of action through their individual passion, vi-sion, and sense of societal priorities. They have changed our insti-tutions, our concepts of gender roles and responsibilities, and the social construction of reality. Indeed, they have been leaders of a different kind. Prompted to action by personal experiences and ob-servation of social injustices against women, they evolved into lead-ers, uniquely supported by colleagues and networks of women with like concerns.

Seldom do their words suggest strong drives for authority and power. While they accepted the importance of platforms, even lobbying mechanisms, they seemed generally to prefer team efforts. While they often acted independently and took risks to promote issues and to advocate solutions, their descriptions emphasize collaboration, networks, and an appreciation for the variety of expertise and insight found within the movement. They were not enamored of institutions or bureaucracies. Frequently they operated from the margins of academic enterprises or they built their own organizations. They took the sights and sounds of the initial stirrings of a chaotic decade and elevated them into a collective dialogue and response that changed and challenged this society's future.

Reflections on Accomplishments

How did these women leaders judge their efforts on behalf of women during the onset and early years of the women's movement? They often spoke about it in very personal terms: "I regained the confidence of my youth through the women's movement. . . . If there hadn't been a women's movement, I would have been a total failure. I can't imagine another constituency or group of bosses or readers or editors who would have thought my work worthwhile. I'm totally dependent on that movement itself, the number of people in it, and also its having changed male thinking on many subjects." Often, these women expressed a sense that what transpired in the early years might not be fully grasped today. One woman observed, for example, that "they don't know that ten years ago [this was all happening for women]—or maybe they know it in their heads but if they didn't live through it, they don't have a sense of what an incredible political struggle went into producing that. And, in a way, it makes it easier for them—that is, they don't feel embattled; they take as a right what we had to struggle for."

The same academic went on to relate an incident she experienced with a woman student in a professional school that captures a sense of the legacy she has transmitted, and the sense that its real meaning may not have registered with the student: "Both of these things were perfectly natural to her, that he should take full cooperation and participation in birth control and that she should be completely and without much consciousness, an equal in professional life. And I had these really mixed feelings. One of them was, 'Well, this is what we fought for.' The other one was, 'Goddamn it! Doesn't she have any sense at all of the agony that went into making this possible and why isn't she out there organizing the women in that field?' "

While our respondents were very articulate about their struggles and some of the pain in the process of changing institutions, they also were very clear about the many accomplishments of the movement. And as they reviewed the movement's outcomes, the general consensus underscores five major accomplishments:

1. Availability of educational and career options (there is general acceptance "that women are not to be denied any opportunity because they are women")

2. Visibility of women in public leadership roles ("the women's movement has given visibility and credibility to a set of issues, problems, worries and doubts that women felt. . . . It has created a collective voice for those doubts about the system"; "there has been a positioning of women in places and institutions that's going to be hard to overturn")

3. Sensitivity to women and the elimination of overt discrimination ("the women's movement has sensitized people not to do the usual putdowns and patronizing things"; "people have become more sensitive to inequalities and cannot make certain statements publicly")

4. Validation of personal experiences and feelings, the collective voice ("I am not alone in feeling discriminated against"; "I do not have to be a superwoman")

5. Expanded role opportunities for both women and men ("as women are doing more things and changing, so are their husbands"; "women sharing in the financial responsibility has taken away the stress from men and it is freeing men to express the nurturing part of their natures [and] it is also giving children the potential of two parents instead of simply one")

Interviews across the three generations suggested that not only has a great deal been achieved, but in no way can we return to where we were before the women's movement. In the words of one leader, "I think we've come to a point where there's no going back. . . . It's too late to lock the door."

The women leaders provided astute analyses of the historical period covering two decades, the 1960s and 1970s, and of the efforts to include women's voices in the public policy arena. Donna E. Shalala, in a speech in 1981 ("Women in Power . . ."), offered the following observations from her experiences as U.S. Undersecretary of Housing and Urban Development under the late Patricia Roberts Harris:

When Secretary Harris came to HUD, there were no programs directed toward women in the matter of housing. There wasn't even much acknowledgment that perhaps women faced special problems when it came to find a place to live. But under Secretary Harris, a full half of the new appointees at HUD went to women. Women were 44 percent of those at executive level. In my own office of policy development and research, half of my new appointments and over half of the senior-level appointments went to women and minorities. . . . The result was immediate. Those women began paying attention to women—to the issues that affected the quality of women's lives in the area of housing. And we made HUD—our institution—pay attention. . . .

We found that women most certainly don't own houses. We discovered that of 48 million owner-occupied homes in the United States, only 18 percent were owned by women and that most of those were over age sixty-five and had presumably inherited ownership through widowhood. . . .

We didn't invent all that. The facts were there, had always been there, hidden. Our administration at HUD was simply the first to see housing as a women's issue. . . . To meet [women's] problems we implemented a review of all housing policies for their impact on [them]. We firmly pointed out the needs of women consumers to industry and to community developers. We came to focus on domestic violence and the need for alternative housing for battered women. We found funds to operate such shelters. . . . Most important of what

happened at HUD was that women were consistently identified as an important constituency group with unique needs in
every one of HUD's major programs and research efforts. And
these needs were only seen when women came into power. . . .

In the process of learning to protect ourselves with our
own expertise, we exercised some of the most important tenets
of the women's movement. Reach out. Build a broad base of
support. . . . The Washington successes and failures were significant learning experiences. For me personally, Washington
whetted my appetite for the long, hard task of reshaping
higher education.

Women with increased self-confidence began to take charge in
shaping the public agenda. Ruth Mandel, in her speech to the American Association of University Women of Pennsylvania in May 1983
("Seize the Day—Women, Politics, and Action"), said: "Perhaps most
important, the proliferation of women's meetings and our growing
concern with the public agenda and public priorities symbolize a
growing self-confidence among women—a rather new type of self-
respect and self-esteem regarding our own capacities for taking charge
. . . not only of our immediate households, our children, our aging
parents, our friends, our jobs, but *also* of the larger public world.
With each passing year we are becoming more confident of our abilities to have an impact on the political process—to vote our minds
and values, and to assume positions of public leadership in our local
communities, in the state, and nationally as well."

Opportunities were opening up for women at all levels, nonetheless slowly and often with little sensitivity to women's needs.
Patricia McPherson, in a dialogue at Mt. Holyoke College titled
"The Revolution Which Should Have Occurred" in the fall of 1984,
said:

Initial consideration of such issues as access to and equity in
higher education leads us to conclude, and properly so, that
much progress has in fact been made. Compare the opportunities for today's high school senior or fledgling college graduate with the opportunities or lack of same which occasioned
the founding of most of the leading women's colleges. . . .

Young women may now apply to virtually all institutions of higher education to become undergraduate or professional school students. They will find most, not all, financial aid and scholarship funds available to those who qualify. Access to programs and equal facilities within the institutions has either been achieved or is in the process of being assured. . . . But on many campuses it was thought not necessary to abolish fraternities, change faculty composition, facilities, or the allocation of real responsibility. Or even to alter the trappings of power. Where changes have occurred, they have come with astonishing slowness and with a surprising lack of sensitivity, given that those mandating the changes could be assumed to have intelligent, even well-educated, wives and daughters.

While our leaders acknowledged many strides forward, they recognize the problems that remain. Willa Player, president emerita of the predominantly black Bennett College, in a speech at the AKA Founders celebration in January 1985 ("Black Women of Power in the Decade of the 80s . . ."), offered the following observations on this point: "Any one of us could compile a small list of horrors illustrating the fact that in spite of the progress we seem to be making women still retain a nebulous, if not subordinate status in society today. This is especially irritating in view of the fact that women constitute a majority of our total population and 93 percent of the enrollment gains in colleges and universities. . . . The important thing to emphasize is that women have become a factor to be reckoned with in our time. . . . Although we are making commendable progress in many areas of life, it is not enough. We are still only tokens. We are still on the periphery—too distant from policy development and decision making. We are still overworked, underpaid, isolated, uncertain, and powerless." While we can document changes made in the home, workplace, and education, the sense conveyed to us was that despite enormous progress, the "revolution" is not over.

One final piece, from a president's platform, serves as a summary statement for many of the women we queried. Donna Shalala cast the accomplishments and agendas of women against the backdrop of George Orwell's *1984*. In her paper titled "Big Sister Is

Watching You: A Feminist View of 1984" presented at the 32nd biennial convention of the American Association of University Women in San Francisco, her forceful comments underscore the dispersion of energies and leadership that flowed from the efforts of the Instigators and Predecessors chronicled earlier:

> Over the past two decades, the women of America have literally transformed our society. We have been entering the labor force in unprecedented numbers—twice the rate of men. In 1950, 35 percent of the adult women in this country worked outside their homes. Today, 59 percent of all women between the ages of 18 and 64 are working outside their homes—nearly 48 million of them.
>
> Many of these women are mothers with children. In 1978, more than half of all mothers with children under 18 were in the labor force. By the year 2000, 75 percent—three out of every four women with children—will be working outside the home.
>
> Clearly these are revolutionary changes not only in the world of work, but in the very lifestyle of people. No doubt about it, we've made progress. But we can't now just sit back and rest on our laurels. . . .
>
> We must not lose our momentum. Our quest to free America of lingering sexism must be multipronged as well as vigorous. Thus, even as we push to improve the pay for work traditionally done by women, we also must expand our options through education; step up our efforts to take jobs that traditionally have been held by men; and aggressively pursue emerging opportunities in the new technologies. Further, we must force a recognition of the tremendous changes wrought by our massive entry into the labor force and try to humanize the workplace by instituting child care, equitable benefits, and flexible schedules which ultimately will benefit everyone—fathers, children, and employers as well as women. . . .
>
> Perhaps a part of what has helped avert the nightmare of *1984* is the Women's Movement. By voting differently from men, women are sending a critical message to the nation. The emerging gender gap is not "just" a vote against sexism. It is

really a proxy for a wide-ranging index of issues. It bespeaks
our growing concern about everything from economic equity
to the health of the environment, our children, social security,
national security, and peace.

The Future Agenda

Assessments lead logically to visions of the future, to work still to
be done, and to experiences of backlash, frustrations, misgivings,
even misinterpretations. The leaders in our study continue to speak
out, often as interpreters of the women's movement's intentions and
accomplishments, past, present, and future. They provide historical
coverage and rich perspectives. One Instigator, for example, offered
these insights:

> I am such an optimist. There's no way you could turn this
> movement back. It is not what happened in the twenties with
> the vote. In the twenties, we had the vote but we didn't have
> an ideology to go with it. What you have now is a well-
> thought-out ideology about a whole variety of women's issues.
> Who would have believed there was a women's issue in trans-
> portation ten years ago? Who would have believed housing is
> a women's issue? Who would believe that technology is a
> women's issue? Computers now have women's issues. Even
> with backlash, even with our losing some issues—and we lose
> some—there's no way that we can go back to where we
> were. . . . There's no way you could turn the clock back any-
> more than if you abolished the Fourteenth Amendment.
> Would we go back to slavery? Of course not. . . . I'm tremen-
> dously optimistic because more and more women know about
> women's issues. They care about them and you have more and
> more sympathetic men.

Public statements convey both the tensions of the 1980s and
some predictions about the future. Juanita Kreps, former dean of
the Women's College at Duke University and a member of the Carter cabinet, at an address at the Texas Foundation for Women's
Resources in November 1984 ("Women Leaders: From Symbols to
Substance"), made these observations:

Tomorrow will bring further progress for American women. Changes will come, however, not in smooth sequence, but in erratic, sometimes unexpected breakthroughs on some fronts, with continued stalemates in others. . . . In any career that women pursue, the hurdles now lie not in gaining access to professions from which we have traditionally been excluded. Young women can realistically expect to compete evenly with men for jobs their mothers (or even their older sisters) never dreamed would be open to them. Rather, the challenge lies in reaching the higher levels of the professions, in gaining leadership roles in the society, where major policies are made— policies that affect the conduct of all institutions, indeed, the conduct of world affairs. In this pursuit, there is a lingering ambivalence that haunts our efforts because we live in a world filled with contradictions. . . . We have one set of rules for getting along in the marketplace and another for getting our work done at home. Technology has supposedly freed us from household drudgery and medical science has extended our life span, yet we never seem to have any free time. We wonder how far we can expect to go and at what pace during this time of transition.

Ellen Futter, president of Barnard College and a lawyer, wife, and mother, provided the following summation of progress made and challenges ahead in a speech given at Pace University, New York, in May 1983 ("Beyond the Superwoman . . ."):

I have specifically advised graduating seniors that they are blessed by having come of age at a time when, as women, they are able to take advantage of and contribute to a society which shall present them with an extraordinary range of opportunities and possibilities. But at the same time, the roles which they may be asked to play will often be in competition with one another and there will, indeed, be times when they question whether it can, in fact, all be done. I have told them, point blank, that I do not really know the answer to this for them, because I believe that the answer varies from individual to individual and changes even within a particular individual's life, depending upon her own development and circumstances at a specific time. I have urged them not to let themselves be trapped into trying to become superwomen—to being all things to all people at one time. The lesson of being a thoroughly modern liberated woman is, at least in part, that of transcending both traditional stereotypes of women's roles in society and more recent, but I believe equally stereotypical, concepts of what women should and should not do with their professional and personal lives.

Felice Schwartz, founder of Catalyst and long an Instigator of changes that support women in the workplace and at home, urged a similar openness to individuality, options, and flexibility in the 1985–1986 annual review of Catalyst titled "Catalyst at 25: Promoting the Potential of Corporate Women."

The feminist movement legitimized the frustration and anger of women about their role in the home but it did not give them the tools to function in new roles. It put legislation in place that forced employers to open their doors to women but it did not help companies to analyze the situation of women, respond to their needs, and bring them up to speed so that they could become a profitable source. And perhaps most notably, it did not significantly alter our perception of what are appropriate roles and behaviors for men and women.

What we must avoid now is our tendency to throw out the baby with the bath water, to limit those options—however inadvertently—that we can make available to women and to men now. It's time to stop wringing our hands about the new problems that confront us—of course, there are problems, there cannot be so massive a change as has taken place without the creation of problems that seem sometimes to overwhelm us.

All three generations of women in the study affirm the existence of an unfinished agenda and persistent frustrations they consider specific to women: (1) continuing and subtle forms of discrimination; (2) confusion and conflict related to feminist identity and philosophy; (3) problems of balance among family, work, and personal agendas; (4) isolation and lack of acceptance within the traditional male hierarchy of institutions and policy groups; and (5) economic issues—from pay inequities and the feminization of poverty to the needs for child care. As these educational leaders envision it, a future agenda would begin by addressing several shared concerns.

Feminism and the New Generation of Women. Respondents indicated some uneasiness about the new generation of professional women not now associated with the women's movement and their seeming lack of a feminist identity in the face of needed momentum for the movement. As we indicated earlier, our leaders felt a lack of recognition on the part of younger women of what the movement has done for them and for women in general, and they are concerned about younger women providing the requisite cadre to carry the torch. In one woman's words, "The graying of the women's movement is worrisome. . . . The young women are the beneficiaries but they take a lot for granted. . . . There is a communication gap—a legacy problem. There is no recognition of the barriers that have been overcome."

While there is a great deal of concern about the lack of a feminist identity among the young professionals, it is also comforting to hear one of the historians in the study remind us that this is what happened in the past after various reform movements: "People who benefit from reform movements rarely understand what it took to get them there. . . . It takes no time for changes to be incorporated and for people to think that it was always there."

Nevertheless, there was agreement among the women in the study that "to keep this second wave of feminism alive it is going to require a lot more vigilance and a lot more maintenance" and that "we need to give younger women the information and survival skills."

Subtle Forms of Discrimination. While there was agreement about having generally been able to overcome overt forms of discrimination, there was also agreement that subtle discrimination continues to exist and to undermine women's self-esteem. An Instigator explained that "the subtle things are terribly important because if you don't know they happen, they damage you, they lower your confidence, they lower your aspirations, they lower your sense of ability to do things. . . . It's the business of knowing you're interrupted. . . . If you don't know that at a conscious level, one cannot help but eventually feel at some level that one is not saying things that are worthwhile." The need to continue to identify discrimination and to develop tactics to combat it rank high among future priorities.

Structural Changes in the Workplace. An assessment of the extent to which real structural changes have not occurred in the workplace troubled the majority of the respondents. While the success of the women's movement is amply demonstrated by women's entry and inclusion in the labor force, the workplace still is organized according to the male model, hierarchical and competitive. Women have had to adapt to that model and have not accomplished the restructure of work to make it easier and less stressful for themselves and, perhaps, for men as well.

We need to recognize the fact that women will continue to opt for marriage and children while pursuing careers. Thus, as long as our conception of careers is based on the male, linear model of progression and success, women will continue to experience stress as they battle to maintain both a family and a career and to establish a sense of personal autonomy. "Time allocations, . . . provisions for helping in career building, . . . need for institutional bending" are all areas that need to be examined and changed. There is a case for "restructuring of the work so that there is not this horrible dichotomy between private life and public life. Child care, relocation, flexible employment patterns, flexible benefits, sexual tension" are all important aspects of the structure of work and each needs to be addressed to "make available to men and women the full array of career and family options."

Economic Issues. The feminization of poverty is a serious priority for the feminist leaders represented in this study. There is agreement that pay inequities and the issues of poor women and comparable worth should be central to an agenda for the coming decades. Donna Shalala, in her paper "Big Sister Is Watching You," says, "One in every three female-headed households is poverty stricken. Predictions are that as this trend continues, by the year 2000, virtually all those living in poverty will be women or children in families headed by women."

Political Power. Perhaps the best way to bring about changes with respect to the issues identified in the feminist agenda is to bring more women into the political power structure. As one respondent said: "The place for women to make themselves felt is in the political arena." Others commented that we have "to draw attention to the need to make changes at the legislative/political level" and that we should get "more women involved in school boards, in state government, in Congress . . . get people into decision-making positions." Often interviewees observed that definitions of success and achievement needed rethinking and redefinition for women to participate fully as leaders in society's institutions and organizations.

We emphasized earlier that the women's movement has reflected differences with respect to the individuals it has attracted to leadership roles and to the issues it attempts to deal with and promote. The women in this study underscore that diversity. While they are quite homogeneous in their professional base and education, their experiences and perceptions differ in ways that reflect the age and social distinctions of the three generations they span.

Questionnaire responses as well as statements made during interview sessions suggest that the Predecessors were most likely to emphasize the necessity of continued work for educational opportunities, both in terms of access and attainment of influential positions. As one Predecessor said, "I don't think all the problems of women are solved by a long shot because . . . I think a lot of the [college and university] searches are phony, and I think the move to the top place is still going to be a carefully guarded spot. I think men are comfortable with women in second place, but I think really significant [college or university] jobs are going to be jealously held on to." The Instigators, on the other hand, invariably focused on the need to obtain greater political power: "Getting a much larger proportion of women into political leadership roles" and "the need to move women into major positions of influence in this faculty" were typical concerns. The Inheritors called attention to the problems of political alienation and backlash and placed a high priority on broadening the base of the women's movement. They seemed especially concerned about the fact that it has been a middle-class movement thus far; they saw a great need to expand the movement to include more women from the lower classes, poor women, older women, and women from diverse ethnic backgrounds. In 1984, Leslie Wolfe, director of the NOW Legal Defense and Education Fund's Project on Equal Education Rights, captured the Inheritors' urgency with regard to overcoming racism in her remarks at the Fifth National Conference of Women in Crisis, New York, in February 1984. In her speech ("Activism in the 80s"), she recalled the leadership of a nineteenth-century heroine, Sojourner Truth:

> In 1867, Sojourner Truth was in her eighties, and had lived forty years a slave in the state of New York and forty years free—and had said that she would be here forty years more to have equal rights for all. She spoke about the bloody battle, recently ended, to win freedom for blacks and said that: "We are now trying for liberty that requires no blood—that women shall have *their* rights—not rights *from* you. Give them what belongs to them; they ask it kindly too. I ask it kindly. Now, I want it done very quick. It can be done in a few years. . . . I don't want to take up your time, but I calculate to live. Now, if you want me to get out of the world, you had better get the women votin' soon. I shan't go till I can do that."
>
> Yes, it is comin'. And it is inevitable. Because, during the past twenty years of feminist activism, we have relearned what our foremothers knew: that there is no such thing as "personal liberation" in a society which discriminates against entire groups of people on the basis of immutable caste factors such as race and sex.

The collective assessment of the issues, outcomes, and commitments on behalf of women over the past two and a half decades provokes some general observations. The leaders in our study spoke of their awareness of a wrong—gender discrimination in education and employment—that they had personally experienced or witnessed in the lives of other women. They talked about sisterhood—the importance of having it and nurturing it in the future. They recognized the necessity for strategies for change. Finally, they advocated an alternative vision of the future in their wish for a society in which women and men work cooperatively to maintain and increase options for work and for personal time and satisfaction.

Equally compelling is the diversity that underlies the momentum and the focus of the women's movement. What surfaces in this study are not only variations in educational and family backgrounds, values, and experiences, but also distinctions in the focus and parameters the women ascribe to the movement itself. While these educational leaders have been involved in the movement for equal rights and for women's liberation, some women have focused their energy primarily in the area of rights, that is, winning legal and economic rights for women, and others have fought and continue to fight for a deeper emancipation—the transformation of institutions and values in our society. The theme of transforming society pervades the comments of many of the leaders, whether they talked about providing a critique of male institutions, questioned success and achievement as they are defined and experienced today, or focused on the importance of restructuring the workplace.

Finally, we offer some observations about the extent to which the past twenty-five years have fulfilled the expectations of the early leaders of the women's movement and also their assessments of the movement's state of health today. Certainly the accounts these women offer do not suggest the death knell of the women's movement nor do they suggest that a fundamental recasting of social structures and roles has been accomplished. In general, the participants in the study are more realistic than pessimistic. While they applaud accomplishments, they recognize not only what remains to be done, but also how difficult success has become. Society is, indeed, more complex, and, after almost three decades, the cumulative issues that affect women's lives today are greater in number and scope. Further, the sheer size and complexity of the movement has exposed important philosophical differences that must be acknowledged and accommodated as work continues.

Complexities and differences associated with a women's agenda invariably increase the demands made on the movement's

leaders. Some persons tend to evaluate the current mood as a dim-
inution of effort and commitment on behalf of women, whereas the
reality may simply be the increased leadership roles women have
assumed. The women in this study whose concerns for human and
civil rights catapulted them into leadership on behalf of women and
equality have now assumed even greater responsibilities in the
search for quality in life and human survival. What they practiced
in the arena of the women's movement has frequently been trans-
ferred to other arenas.

The comments, beliefs, values, and hopes expressed through
these women leaders argue for a continued, perhaps more calculated, effort on behalf of women. Women from all walks of life must
be included in planning and implementing an agenda that speaks
to the range and complexity of issues that demand attention.

The setting of an agenda demands unity on perhaps the most
fundamental issues:

- The identification and nurturance of the next generation of
  feminists
- The restructuring of work to enhance the human potential of
  both women and men and to increase the realization of quality
  in all aspects of human existence
- The eradication of discrimination against women as it appears
  in its more subtle and insidious forms
- The attainment of political and economic power that allows
  leadership on the part of women to reach its full potential far
  beyond the tokenism extended over the past twenty-five years

The understanding available in this study holds much prom-
ise for addressing the challenges of the future. Generational perspectives and the assessments of the leaders who initiated efforts on
behalf of women strengthen both the integrity of the women's
movement and the urgency of its future.

CHAPTER 9

A Leadership Legacy,
A Leadership Resource

I think I feel very fortunate. I have influenced, literally, the lives of millions of people.

—Instigator

Our study was designed to examine leadership from a woman's perspective and to expand our notions about leadership beyond
"conventional" views. Grounded on the premise that knowledge is
socially constructed, in that it is dependent on a social, cultural, and
historical context, the study explores the experience and leadership across three generations of seventy-seven women educational
leaders.

Overview

Recognizing that leadership can be both positional and nonpositional, we studied women who held highly visible positions, such
as college and university presidents, as well as women who have
changed institutions and affected legislation through their scholarly endeavors—leaders who integrated their political activism with
their intellectual work and advocated institutional transformation
through their scholarship. To understand leadership succession and
leadership within different cultural and historical contexts, we selected the women for the study from three different generations—

women who were active professionally as early as the 1940s—the Predecessors; women who instigated change during the second wave of the women's movement, the Instigators; and the Inheritors, women who are building on the legacy of the first two groups and who have more recently come into their own as leaders.

We have chosen to view leadership as integral to social change and as a creative process that empowers others to organize collectively for action. The data gathered suggest a conceptual model of leadership that comprises two major aspects: the outcomes of leadership and the processes involved in achieving those outcomes. While the conceptual framework that guided the analysis and interpretation of the primary and secondary sources of data was derived primarily from feminist discourse about human phenomena, empirical data enabled us to propose a model as a useful approach for examining leadership. The model identifies four key elements in any study of leadership: (1) the leader, (2) the context, (3) the leadership processes, and (4) the outcomes. We have focused on outcomes because we view leadership as a change process—in this case social transformation that has brought women and their concerns closer to the center of human activities. Processes include the style and strategies leaders employ in empowering others toward collective action.

The study was designed to learn about leadership in a social movement. While it is an analysis of leadership outcomes and processes, it is also a narrative presentation of people and events in three decades spanning the onset and evolution of the modern women's movement. Personal interviews and questionnaires provide primary data sources. Secondary data sources include speeches, autobiographical accounts, and other writing by the women leaders. These data offer a record of events too seldom noted but so often critical to opportunities we now take for granted.

In undertaking this study our aim was to expand our knowledge of leadership talent as represented by women educators—populations (both women and educators) that have been left out of most of the previous studies on leadership. We chose each woman for our sample because she had accomplished visible, sometimes multiple changes on behalf of women. The contributions of the leaders we studied include the elimination of overt forms of gender discrimination, the increased visibility of women in public leadership roles, the expansion of educational and career options for women, the greater flexibility of roles for both women and men, and the validation of personal experiences and emotions. Our subjects created new organizations such as Catalyst, a New York–based organization devoted to improving women's access and progress within the business sector, and the Feminist Press—a publishing house devoted to the publication and distribution of materials for and about women. They were the women who started and developed continuing education programs, women's studies programs, centers for research on women, and journals such as *Signs*. They provided crucial leadership in drafting the passage of affirmative action legislation. In sum, their efforts on behalf of women brought about significant reforms in legislation and other areas of society, and generated new knowledge that is being incorporated into academic disciplines and curricula.

As we review the study's findings, three elements emerge as significant factors in these leadership accomplishments: collective action, passionate commitment, and consistent performance.

Collective Action. Virtually all of the women in the study conceive of leadership as a process of "working with people and through people." They constantly acknowledge the thoughts and energies of others who helped them or who laid the groundwork for their labors: "Things that I accomplished . . . not one of them did I accomplish alone. . . . There were other women working with me." They use power collectively: "Change occurs by hard work, by inspiring people to form a vision, by networking, and by having people come together to accomplish a change."

Passionate Commitment. As agents of social change, these leaders took action because of an acute awareness of injustices in our society. They share a strong commitment to social justice and change. As veterans of numerous social movements and causes— labor, peace, civil rights, antiwar, wages, housing, jobs, education—many of them took advantage of or created opportunities to solve problems and to make a difference. Their passion comes in part from direct personal experiences: experiencing or witnessing discrimination. Their values stem from their roots: grandparents, parents, or other relatives who also cared passionately about social justice.

Consistent Performance. How did they go about initiating change? First, they identified problems and accepted complexity as both a challenge and an opportunity. They developed a network of like-minded people and worked together within and outside the system to transform it. Their specific qualities and strategies emphasize clarity of values, listening to and empowering others, and doing one's homework. Their styles rely greatly on self-awareness and on interpersonal and communication skills.

John Gardner (1990, p. 119) indicates that for leaders to function in the complex world of today they need critically important skills that involve agreement building, networking, the exercise of nonjurisdictional power, and institution building. Our leaders indeed demonstrate these skills. They are agreement builders: "To change things at the university it required that faculty and students united." "The way to make a decision and make it stick is to listen to all constituents." They network: "Change occurs by hard work, by inspiring people to form a vision, by networking and having people come together to accomplish change." "We had power jointly as a group." They exercise nonjurisdictional power: "Command isn't leadership. Command you get by virtue of your office. Anybody can command who's got the office." "I am not hierarchical. I'm much more comfortable by trying to create consensus. I may say that we as a goup have to do something." They are institution builders by empowering their co-workers: "Your job is to get them to do their best. . . . You have got to make them feel good in order to get them to be effective." "I believe so strongly in delegation and I believe so strongly in letting people move it along as far as they can, I am a delegator and a supporter." "I am interested in enabling very good people to do their work with great freedom."

Our study extends the study of leadership and the development of theory, first through a focus on outcomes and processes, and second by providing data for a significant leader population—women—that allow us to analyze the operational realities of major leadership concepts: change, empowerment, and collective action.

At the same time, this investigation raises many questions that should be pursued in the future.

Future Directions

In designing the study we were guided by the belief that more attention needed to be focused on the *function* of leadership as opposed to the formal *role* of the leader. Even though we felt constrained, as others have been, by the traditional conceptions of leadership—the notion that there is a person, "the leader," who is supposed to behave in certain ways and to demonstrate certain skills—we tried to focus more on the process by which effective leadership achieves certain outcomes. The experience of conducting this study has convinced us that in future research on leadership much more attention should be devoted to the processes involved in achieving desired leadership outcomes.

To understand the leadership process we need to design studies that identify the mechanisms by which people become empowered. Unless group members believe in themselves and feel powerful, it will be difficult for them to participate collectively— a necessary condition to achieve change in organizations or in society. Thus in order to further enhance our understanding of the processes of empowerment and collective action, we would like to recommend that future studies on leadership be designed to consider two critical dimensions:

1. If leadership means a process of change (leadership to some end), then we need to understand the antecedents of activism and passionate commitment. What experiences in the home or school develop commitment and a sense of urgency?

2. If leadership is collective action, then we need to design studies that examine the motivation for and dynamics of collective behavior. We need to ask questions such as the following: How does collaboration begin? How is it sustained? How do individuals coalesce? And, how does the concept of collaboration become valued by individual group members?

Since most of the research and publications on leadership have focused on the formal role of "leader" within hierarchically structured organizations, we need to study nontraditional and nonhierarchical organizations such as community action groups, voluntary organizations, musical ensembles, dance companies in order to expand our understanding of leadership and our ability to develop effective leaders. Future studies should look at horizontally structured organizations or groups and examine leadership as exercised by collective action.

And now a word about methodology. While studies of leadership have often been based on individual interviews and questionnaires, we see great merit in the use of biography and autobiography as a means of understanding the antecedents of activism and passion—the driving forces in leadership behavior. Further, we believe that participant observation and ethnography should be seriously considered in studies of leadership because they represent methodologies that can inform us about the processes of empowerment and collective action.

Implications for Leadership Development

From chronicling the dynamics and accomplishments of this remarkable group of women, we are struck by two distinct but interrelated processes in the arena of leadership development and utilization. These are the task of identifying and educating new generations of leaders, and the task of utilizing the reservoir of experienced leaders to meet the emerging issues confronting society.

Developing the Next Generation of Leaders. Our Predecessors, Instigators, and Inheritors underscore the fact that important linkages and transitions can be made between leadership generations. The Predecessors, for example, provided a legacy of their own in laying important groundwork within institutional structures, building platforms and visibility for women, and modeling competence, hard work, and professional presence. Once again, they remind us of the importance of role models and mentors and of the personal support one leadership generation can provide to enable its successors.

Similarly, we note in our Instigators an emphasis on teaching as well as mentoring or coaching a new leadership cohort. Their experiences help us to understand what it takes to be a social change agent. Conferences, forums, and projects that mix generations of leaders offer a means of transmitting knowledge and values that can encourage the passion of the Inheritors. Such exchanges were well documented in this study. The women leaders who spoke through these pages never hesitated to admit that they could not have accomplished their goals without the encouragement and guidance of others. These findings argue for leadership education that involves active learning, the participation of future leaders in purposeful activities where they can test competencies, take risks, manifest values, and simultaneously receive support, counsel, and validation from more experienced leaders.

In sum, we applaud and encourage leadership development that pays conscious attention to the critical dimension of succession, capitalizes on the rich opportunities of interdependence by linking leadership generations, and utilizes the teaching role for seasoned leaders to transmit their knowledge about leadership and to mentor their successors through active learning experiences. In such activities we recognize the power of Erik Erikson's (1980) concept of generativity and its potential achievement through intergenerational relations. We see the special, crucial role that leaders who have "arrived" in their positions play in sharing responsibility and authority with their successors. This study allows us to consider Erickson's notion at a slightly different level—the generativity of a collective whose turning over of leadership responsibilities and political legacy should mean more than the symbolic passing of the torch.

Our study makes clear that leadership cannot prosper fully as a solitary phenomenon. On the contrary, the most experienced leaders in our sample—the Predecessors and Instigators—needed opportunities for colleagueship that promote the sharing of wisdom and insight, away from the heated battles of the activism they generated. As a society, we cannot afford to assume that dialogue and colleagueship always follow such activism and leadership. Yet, we need the insights continued discourse among leaders might offer.

Sustaining the Current Leadership Resource. Our research confirms the existence of a significant reservoir of experienced leadership talent and expertise for the next century. The questions the study provoke are these: How can we as a society sustain and extend such a leadership resource? How can we reward and capitalize on the wisdom and experience of the leadership cohorts who have served with passion and excellence?

We do not mean to suggest that many of these women leaders do not continue to provide leadership talents beyond their previously noted or visible leadership roles. The study offers many instances of research, writing, community service, board memberships, and participation on government task forces that utilize our leaders' talents and personal energy. The study did let us see, nonetheless, the subtle but substantial personal drain on the women, particularly on the Instigators, whose activism forged new societal perspectives but less often attracted recognition or support for replenishment or the redirection of their talents to other fields or issues. If we are to sustain leaders with their creative energies and vision, then we should be more deliberate about it. We need not only invite and encourage them to contribute further to emerging societal concerns or innovative opportunities. We should provide mechanisms that facilitate their participation and make it possible for them to do so.

We found in our data ample justification for rethinking leadership development to include specific actions that support such collective generativity. In many instances, our higher education system and other programs provide support and encouragement for young investigators and emerging leaders—our Inheritor cohort. We need only think of the many postdoctoral fellowship programs for researchers or the highly visible leadership development fellowships provided by major philanthropies such as the Kellogg Foundation or the Danforth Foundation. These programs have made major contributions to the identification and encouragement of future leaders in this country. If we take the concept of development seriously, however, attention and concern for professional enhancement and growth for leaders must be across the life span. As the life span has stretched so, too, have our leadership resources.

Institutions and organizations need to tap the resources of a mature leadership cohort and to provide new roles to involve experienced voices. We need to assist them with transitions, and encourage them to engage in dialogue, teaching, mentoring, and coaching of new cohorts of potential leaders. In some instances, this could mean doing more of what some institutions are now doing in inviting emeritae professors to continue with research and teaching. But it also calls for a more deliberate effort to sustain women leaders, particularly those from the social and political arenas—through stipends, fellowships, and travel, without the need for endless application forms and reviews.

We urge more creative and generous rethinking of the rewards, recognition, and replenishment we offer our leaders. We would like to see opportunities for individuals to plan for successive stages in their leadership development in ways that will satisfy their personal interests and goals while at the same time contributing to organizations and institutions.

Inevitably, support to pursue research, writing, and teaching, or to develop special community service projects, may require financial support. As a minimum, it will necessitate some different configurations within institutions to accommodate persons who may not always fit neatly into academic enclaves. If as a society we value leadership talent and we recruit and nurture it with care in the early stages of career development, surely we should be perceptive enough and willing to enable leaders to fulfill their individual capacities and realize their fullest contributions to our society, throughout their lifetimes.

Our study has helped us learn about the practice and the study of leadership and about how women function as leaders. We hope that this study attracts others to further research on the topic, to possible new directions for programs to develop leadership talent, and to ways we can assess leadership behaviors and outcomes.

The study has been both an inquiry into the phenomenon of leadership and a celebration of a group of women who through enormous wisdom and personal courage have made a difference in our lives. As their life stories have inspired us, we hope that our account of their contributions will inspire our readers and future generations of Inheritors to continue the legacy of leadership to improve life for all people, everywhere.

RESOURCE

Background Documents

List of Participants

Florence Anderson
Former Executive Secretary
Carnegie Corporation

Alberta Arthurs
Director for Arts and
    Humanities
Rockefeller Foundation

Patricia Bell-Scott
Professor of Human
    Development and Family
    Relations
University of Connecticut

Jessie Bernard
Research Scholar Honoris
    Causa
Pennsylvania State University

Alison Bernstein
Program Officer
Ford Foundation

Laura Bornholdt
Special Assistant to the
    President
University of Chicago

Janet Welsh Brown
Senior Associate
World Resources Institute

Mary I. Bunting
President Emerita
Radcliffe College

Cecilia Preciado Burciaga
Senior Associate Provost
Stanford University

Jean Campbell
Former Director
Center for Continuing
    Education of Women
University of Michigan

Mary Ellen Capek
Executive Director
National Council for Research
    on Women

Mariam Chamberlain
Founding President and
    Resident Scholar
National Council for Research
    on Women

167

Elizabeth Cless
Founder and Former Director
PLATO Society
UCLA Extension

Audrey Cohen
President and Founder
College of Human Services

Jill Ker Conway
President Emerita
Smith College

Marsha Jean Darling
Faculty Fellow, Division of
Community Life
Smithsonian Institution

Opal David
Former Director
Commission on the Education
of Women ACE

Margaret Dunkle
Executive Director
Equality Center

Carolyn Elliot
Vice Provost
University of Vermont

Alice F. Emerson
President
Wheaton College

Sara Englehardt
Executive Vice President
Foundation Center

Cynthia Fuchs Epstein
Professor of Sociology,
Graduate Center
CUNY Graduate School

Gail Fullerton
President
San Jose State University

Ellen Futter
President
Barnard College

Sister Ann Ida Gannon, B.V.M.
President Emerita
Mundelein College

Carol Gilligan
Professor of Human
Development and Psychology
Harvard Graduate School of
Education

Patricia Albjerg Graham
Dean of School of Education
Harvard University

Hannah Holborn Gray
President
University of Chicago

Evelyn Handler
President
Brandeis University

Matina Horner
President Emerita
Radcliffe College

Lilli Hornig
Former Director
HERS–New England

Florence Howe
Director
Feminist Press
City University of New York

Arlene Johnson
Senior Research Associate
Work and Family Center
Catalyst

Nannerl Keohane
President
Wellesley College

Juanita Kreps
James B. Duke Professor of
    Economics
and Vice President Emerita
Duke University

Gerda Lerner
Robinson-Edwards Professor of
    History
University of Wisconsin–
    Madison

Jean Lipman-Blumen
Thornton F. Bradshaw
    Professor of Public Policy
Claremont Graduate School

Rosalind Loring
Former Director
Daytime Programs for Women
University of California, Los
    Angeles/Extension

Mary McPherson
President
Bryn Mawr College

Sister Colette Mahoney
President Emerita
Marymount Manhattan College

Ruth Mandel
Director
Center for the American
    Woman and Politics
Rutgers University

Jacqueline Mattfeld
Vice Provost
Arizona State University–West
    Campus

Mary Metz
President
Mills College

Mary Ann Millsap
Senior Research Associate
National Institute of Education

Kathryn Moore
Professor of Education
    Administration
Michigan State University

Barbara W. Newell
Chancellor
State University System of
    Florida

Jean O'Barr
Director
Women's Studies
Duke University

Rosemary Park
President Emerita
Barnard College

Sherry Penney
Chancellor
University of Massachusetts–
    Boston

Martha Peterson
President Emerita
Beloit College

Patti McGill Peterson
President
Wells College

Willa Player
President Emerita
Bennett College

Deborah S. Rosenfelt
Professor and Women's Studies
    Director
University of Maryland

Alice Rossi
Harriet Martineau Professor of
    Sociology
University of Massachusetts–
    Amherst

Mary Rowe
Special Assistant to the
    President
MIT

Bernice Resnick Sandler
Director
Project on the Status and
    Education of Women
Association of American
    Colleges

Marcia Savage
President
Manhattanville College

Nancy Schlossberg
Professor
College of Education
University of Maryland

Felice Schwartz
President
Catalyst

Anne Firor Scott
W. K. Boyd Professor of History
Duke University

Joan Wallach Scott
Professor of Social Science
Institute for Advanced Studies

Cynthia Secor
Director
HERS, Mid-America
University of Denver, Colorado
    Women's College Campus

Donna Shalala
Chancellor
University of Wisconsin–
  Madison

Donna Shavlik
Director
Office of Women in Higher
  Education
American Council on
  Education

Adele Simmons
President
MacArthur Foundation

Virginia Smith
Former President
Vassar College

Catharine Stimpson
University Professor, Dean of
  the Graduate School,
and Vice Provost for Graduate
  Education
Rutgers University

Carol Stoel
Director
AAUW Educational
  Foundation

Emily Taylor
Senior Associate
Office of Women in Higher
  Education
American Council on
  Education

M. Elizabeth Tidball
Professor of Physiology
George Washington University
  Medical Center

Irene Tinker
Professor of City and Regional
  Planning and Women's
  Studies
University of California,
  Berkeley

Sheila Tobias
Author and Professor of
  Political Science
University of Arizona

Barbara Uehling
Chancellor
UC Santa Barbara

Mary Lindenstein Walshok
Associate Vice Chancellor
UC San Diego

Jean Walton
Vice President for Student
  Affairs, Emerita
Pomona College

Margaret Wilkerson
Professor and Chair, Afro-
  American Studies
University of California,
  Berkeley

Leslie Wolfe
Executive Director
Center for Women Policy
  Studies

Speeches and Presentations from Participants

Bunting, M. I. "Education and Evolution." Convocation address, Vassar College, Oct. 1961.

Bunting, M. I. "The University's Responsibility in Educating Women for Leadership." Speech at Southern Methodist University, Jan. 1966.

Bunting, M. I. "Women: Resource for a Changing World." Address at invitational conference, Radcliffe College, Apr. 1972.

Futter, E. "Beyond the Superwoman: Woman's Education in the 1980s." Speech at Pace University, New York, May 5, 1983.

Kreps, J. "Women Leaders: From Symbols to Substance." Address at Texas Foundation for Women's Resources, Nov. 1984.

McPherson, M. P. "The Revolution Which Should Have Occurred." A dialogue at Mt. Holyoke College, Fall 1984.

Mandel, R. "Seize the Day—Women, Politics and Action." Speech to the American Association of University Women of Pennsylvania, May 1983.

Player, W. "Black Women of Power in the Decade of the 80s Challenge: The Making of a Leader." Speech at AKA Founders Celebration, Jan. 1985.

Schlossberg, N. K. "Rumblings of a Mad Feminist." Paper presented at meeting of the American Council on Education, May 1974.

Schwartz, F. "Women in the Workforce: Making the Most of a Bonanza and Making It Work for Families." Keynote address at Women's Career Center, Rochester, N.Y., 1985.

Shalala, D. E. "Women in Power: A Feminist Agenda for the 1980s." Speech at the International Interdisciplinary Congress on Women, Haifa, Israel, Dec. 1981.

Shalala, D. E. "Big Sister Is Watching You: A Feminist View of

1984." Paper presented at 32nd biennial convention of the American Association of University Women, San Francisco, June 1983.

Tidball, M. E. "Toward Developing a Common Perspective." Speech at inauguration of president of Russell Sage College, Oct. 1976.

Wolfe, L. R. "Activism in the 80's." Speech at the fifth national conference of Women in Crisis, Inc., New York, Feb. 1984.

Wingspread Conference Proposal

Purposes

To convene a representative group of women leaders from education, the government/political arena, communications media, and business/industry whom we have designated as *instigators** because of the initiatives they took in the late 1960s and early 1970s

To discuss personal and social issues pertinent to recognizing and developing women's leadership for the future

To generate a statement on national needs and opportunities for leadership which will guide policy makers in education, government, and philanthropic organizations over the next decade

Rationale

There is a somewhat understandable but nonetheless disconcerting lull in the interest and emphasis on the special needs or concerns of women. That does not mean important activities aren't happening; they are. Curricular change, publications, research, and recruitment and training efforts have taken a firm hold in several major institutions and systems. But, the gains toward equal access and

---

*By *instigator* we mean a woman who assumed a visible leadership role on behalf of women between 1965 and 1975 through one or more of the following means: developing funding programs within the government or foundations geared to achieving equity for women; publishing and/or distributing feminist literature and information about women's positions and roles in education; formulating legislation affecting the lives of women, and so forth.

participation for women do not represent an end to the problems they face in our society. Just as the times have changed, so have the problems. As we witness new national priorities and leadership needs, for example, there are some who question whether women are among those who will be available, willing, and prepared to accept major leadership roles.

Current worldwide economic and political issues may justifiably overshadow a number of individual or organizational situations, and the general recession-ridden state of affairs often makes it difficult to single out any one constituency for attention. The underlying uneasiness which motivates this proposal, however, is that the momentum of the women's movement and the strength of its leadership cohort could too easily be lost in a shuffle of national resources and priorities. The time seems particularly ripe to (1) take stock of what has transpired as a result of initiatives focused on women in the late 1960s, early 1970s, and (2) set an agenda of policy and leadership emphases for both short- and long-term planning. The challenge underscores a need for some visionary observations and projections about women and leadership in our society which offer perspective and direction to educational policy-makers in the next decade and beyond. It is to that challenge that this proposal is addressed.

The women who took initiatives and risks over the past two decades are not only still available to us, but constitute a very special resource. Their accomplishments have been documented and their influence has been felt through the structures they developed, the writings they produced, and the leadership in national and international deliberations they have provided. We believe they can make an important contribution to an agenda in these pre-1984 election months which speaks to continued attention to women's lives, to revitalization of education and training, and to the place of women in the leadership of this country.

Participants and Format

Twenty women who are part of the instigator group will be invited to participate in working sessions for two days. The focus of discussions will be leadership in the next decade: what needs to be done, what kinds of leaders we need to do it, and what needs those leaders have. Parameters for the discussion, in both the full group and small work groups, will be provided by provocateurs who will prepare pre-retreat materials to stimulate thinking and raise questions which tap the experiences and perspectives of the women to be involved.

All sessions will be taped and from the proceedings, and a document will be produced for circulation among educational associations, institutions, government agencies, and other appropriate organizations such as foundations and nonprofit groups. A backward glance over the past twenty years of the women's movement underscores how many activities and research efforts were triggered by small conferences and deliberations: the American Council on Education Policy Statement in 1960, the Report of the President's Commission on the Status of Women and the Itasca conference, both in 1963, the *Daedalus* papers in 1964, and the MIT symposium on women in science. We feel such a statement is currently in order.

The Johnson Foundation has agreed to provide the conference facilities of Wingspread for two and one-half days for twenty participants and five facilitators/provocateurs. The conference is scheduled to be convened November 13–15 at Racine, Wisconsin.

Helen S. Astin
Carole Leland
April 1983

Framework for Discussion

1. *Retrospective*

- Key elements in our successes or our failures
- What has worked in the past?
- What have been critical incidents or variables related to our and others' leadership?
- What have we learned?
- The roots and consequences of backlash

2. *Forms and Arenas for Leadership*

- Linking women across race, ethnic, and class lines
- International bridges—role of U.S. movement in the international scene
- Power and potential of women's organizations
- Girls—are we forgetting them in youth programs, in education, and in the women's movement?
- By what process or through what vehicles do women harness the energy they innately have, for example, through government service, politics, organizations, or institutions?
- What kinds of linkages are appropriate, necessary, vital to women leaders?

3. *Transmitting Our Recollections: The Inheritors*

- How do we identify, recruit, and nurture leadership talent?
- How do we build the environment and support for promising women that they will perceive as sustaining their ambitions and sufficient to overcome the real emotional setback dealt by a male-powered culture?
- Who are our inheritors and what can we observe about their aspirations, strategies, and needs?

- Is it possible that shortsighted ambitions to get ahead are caus-ing careful male-like behavior that in the long run could leave us with a lot of middle (and middling) managers who find greater reward in security than in the risks of leadership?
- How and where do we make generation bridges?

4.   Constraints and Resistance

- What are the problems we encounter with women's leadership now, and what can we anticipate in the next decades?
- Male-female partnerships or competitions?
- Media-fueled backlash against successful, executive women
- When you empower self, what happens to sisterhood?
- Implications and responsibilities vis-à-vis the "gender gap"
- Pay equity and fringe benefits and the dilemma of the female-headed household
- Whose executive are you, anyway? The complex relationship between female executives and traditionally male-dominated boards

5.   Strategies for Coping and Sustaining

- Why do the strides we have made as women seem to be two steps forward and then one backward—is there anything we can do to effect a change in this pattern?
- How do we sustain ourselves and others in leadership roles?
- What kind of support do we need and how do we get it?
- How do we diffuse (and de-fuse?) the impact of a shift of lead-ership in a variety of sectors and at many levels into the hands of women? How do we make it acceptable to those whose power is diluted?
- How do we contain and moderate the ricochet against women? How do we present what may become a we-win/you-lose contest so that, instead, it is seen as a process in which we all win?
- How can we get foundations to be interested in women's issues in general?
- What strategies are most likely to have the "biggest bang for the buck"?
- How can we utilize the "gender gap" as leverage for funding and for change?

- How do we balance personal enhancement and social issues?
- What can be done about the lack of women in influential roles in the media—the lack of women directors in film and women executive producers in television?

6. *Allocating Energies for the Future*

- Women and the new technology: how the computer age will impact women in social, psychological, and political terms, as well as in career terms
- Postfeminism—does it exist?
- What's the "cutting edge"—how do we move into new topics, new arenas?
- What roles need to be taken now by our leadership cohort?
- What are the priorities for individual and collective energies?

Summary of Interview Protocol

Each interview consists of a structured format that addresses five major domains: (1) *social context and issues,* (2) *leadership,* (3) *peer and work relationships,* (4) *personal and professional development,* and (5) *issues and legacies of the women's movement.*

Interviews focus on the five preceding areas but are idiosyncratic in keeping with each participant's particular role and/or special contribution to education. All interviews were audiotaped and were conducted by one of the principal coinvestigators, both of whom have extensive training in counseling psychology and interviewing. During the initial interviewing phases, several interviews were conducted jointly to establish interjudge reliability. The protocol, currently in use and therefore not published for wider distribution, includes:

1. *Social Context and Issues*

- Establishes role(s) and activities of participant in period of early 1960s, with special reference to the issues and concerns of the women's movement
- Focuses on critical incidents that provoked involvement in particular social causes (for example, civil rights, antiwar activities, women's movement, and so on)
- Ascertains values and commitments to particular issues, including background (family, ethnic, religious), events (childhood, college, postcollege)
- Elicits experiences in causes or movements, including personal objectives and strategies to accomplish them; involvement, support, or resistance from others; and perceptions of general activities and involvement of others

2. *Leadership*

- Identifies antecedents: childhood, adolescent, and college experiences; specific roles; and extent of participation
- Obtains personal attributes, positive and negative; styles and strategies used in various leadership contexts, especially in bringing about change; and critical events in developing current leadership style
- Discusses mentors and role models (male or female), influential through observation, direct coaching, or vicariously; descriptive assessments and assessment of power and influence available and exercised (with illustrations)

3. *Peer and Work Relationships*

- Examines interaction and communication with same- and opposite-gender work associates, quality of interaction, sense of personal acceptance and contribution in varied contexts, nature of support, extent and focus of discussions, quality of working relationships
- Reveals comparisons with opposite-gender leadership styles and effectiveness; networking and the need for and availability of colleagueship and support groups or individuals; and significant peers whose leadership has brought about change

4. *Personal and Professional Development*

- Inspects cost/demands and benefits/satisfactions of leadership experiences; frustrations/obstacles in bringing about objectives or changes; supportive or facilitating factors; and specific alterations or abandonment of plans and objectives
- Reviews personal support—staff, partner/spouse, friends (male or female), and extent of shared commitments to issues or activities; relationship of personal life to professional responsibilities; nature of visibility and demands—complementary and/or competing; replenishment, sources for recharging (for example, leisure, recreation activities, social life, spiritual and/or religious involvement); health, energy level, personal needs for time, schedule, and so on; past and present impact on self directly or indirectly as related to significant others

- Scrutinizes professional agenda, career plans and aspirations from present situation; issues or activities that seem attractive or challenging; roles that might be played in the future; and talents, experiences, commitments that might be societal resources

5. *Issues and Legacies of the Women's Movement*

- Assesses events and outcomes over past ten to twenty years; issues that have been important, remain important, and so on; personal involvement or priorities past, present, and future with an emphasis on continuities and discontinuities; nature of legacy from the women's movement; and inheritors of leadership responsibilities and commitment vis-à-vis women's issues
- Examines male-female differences in priority issues and interactions and bridges inheritor generation

Women Educational Leaders: Participant Profile

1. Your name (please print): _____
   (Last)   (First)   (Middle/Maiden)

2. Date of Birth ____ / ____ / _____
   Mo.   Day   Year

3. Place of Birth: _____
   City   State   Country

4. Community in which you spent most of your growing up years (circle one).

   Farm or open country 1
   Town of less than 10,000 population 2
   Town of 10,000–49,999 population 3
   Suburb or central city of metropolitan area
      of less than 100,000 population 4
      of 100,000 to 499,999 population 5
      of 500,000 to 2 million population 6
      of more than 2 million population 7

5. How many times did your family move during your childhood years?

      None 1
      Once 2
      Twice 3
      Three times 4
      Four times 5
      Five or more 6

This research is being conducted under the auspices of the Higher Education Research Institute, The University of California at Los Angeles, and is funded in part by the Ford Foundation and the Exxon Education Foundation. Principal Investigators are Helen S. Astin, Ph.D., and Carole Leland, Ph.D.

183

6.   Marital/Partner Status (circle all that apply).

      Single (never married) 1   *Indicate Year Below:*
      Married 2   _____
      Remarried 3   _____
      Separated 4   _____
      Divorced 5   _____
      Widowed 6   _____
      Intimate Partner 7   _____

7.   Children: *Ages*   *Ages*

      Male   adopted ___ ___ ___   biological ___ ___ ___
      Female   adopted ___ ___ ___   biological ___ ___ ___

8.   Highest level of education completed by your present spouse/ partner (circle one).

      Less than high school 1
      High school graduate 2
      Some college 3
      College graduate 4
      Some graduate school 5
      Graduate or professional degree 6
      Specify: _____

9.   Spouse/partner occupation (specify): _____

10.   Highest level of education attained by parents (circle one for each):

                                       Mother   *Father*

      Grammar school 1   1
      Some high school 2   2
      High school graduate 3   3
      Some college or other school 4   4
      College graduate 5   5
      Some graduate school 6   6
      Graduate or professional degree 7   7
      Specify: _____

11.   What was your father's principal occupation? Specify: _____

12. Was your mother employed while you were growing up (circle one)?

No 1
Yes 2

13. If yes, was most of your mothers's employment (circle one):

Part-time? 1
Full-time? 2

14. What was your mother's principal occupation? Specify: ____

15. Indicate the state or foreign country in which your parents were born:

Father _____ Mother _____

16. What is your birth order position (circle one)?

First born and only 1
First born 2
Second born 3
Third or later born 4

17. Number of siblings: Brother(s) ____ Sister(s) ____

18. What type of high school did you attend (circle one)?

Public 1
Private 2

19. Information about educational attainment (If desired, attach resume):

	Year Awarded	Major Field	College/ University
Bachelor's	_____	_____	_____
	_____	_____	_____
Master's	_____	_____	_____
	_____	_____	_____

Doctorate   _____   _____   _____

                  _____   _____   _____

Professional   _____   _____   _____

                  _____   _____   _____

Honorary   _____   _____   _____
degree(s)
                  _____   _____   _____

                  _____   _____   _____

                  _____   _____   _____

                  _____   _____   _____

20. List the *three* positions you held prior to your current posi-
     tion. (Attach resume, if desired)

Title/		*Dates*
Rank	*Name of Institution/Organization*	*From–To*
_____	_____	_____
_____	_____	_____
_____	_____	_____

21. What is your present occupation/position?

Title/		
Rank	*Name of Institution/Organization*	*Date*
_____	_____	_____
_____	_____	_____

22. What is your current salary/retirement income?

              Less than $20,000 1
              $20,000–$29,000 2
              $30,000–$39,000 3
              $40,000–$49,000 4

$50,000-$59,000 5
$60,000 plus 6

23. Approximately how much income did you receive last year from royalties, lecturing, consulting, and honoraria:

None 1
Less than $1,000 2
$1,000-$4,999 3
$5,000-$9,999 4
$10,000 plus 5

24. How would you consider your health at present?

Poor 1
Fair 2
Good 3
Excellent 4

25. Have you had any major illnesses (circle one)?

No 1
Yes 2

26. If yes, please indicate the years of illness: _____ _____

27. *To what extent* have major illnesses or health factors of others (relative/partner) affected your life (circle one)?

No 1
Slight 2
Moderate 3
Considerable 4
Great 5

28. Religious background/preference (circle one in each column):

	Religion you were raised in	*Current religious preference*
None	1	1
Protestant	2	2

Catholic 3 3
Jewish 4 4
Other 5 5
Specify: _____   _____

29. List the professional, volunteer, and women's organizations
     in which you have served or are serving (e.g., corporate or
     institutional boards, discipline associations, community
     agencies, etc.):

Professional Organization Name	Years	Role/Title
_____	_____	_____
_____	_____	_____
_____	_____	_____
_____	_____	_____

Name of Volunteer Organization	Years	Role/Title
_____	_____	_____
_____	_____	_____
_____	_____	_____
_____	_____	_____

Women's Organization Name	Years	Role/Title
_____	_____	_____
_____	_____	_____
_____	_____	_____
_____	_____	_____

30. How would you rate yourself on the following personal characteristics?

<table>
<tr><td></td><td>Low</td><td></td><td></td><td>High</td></tr>
<tr><td></td><td>1</td><td>2</td><td>3</td><td>4</td><td>5</td></tr>
</table>

Humor .... ——
Creativity .... ——
Ambition .... ——
Self-confidence .... ——
Adaptability .... ——
Physical appearance .... ——
Independence .... ——
Risk-taking .... ——
Interpersonal skills .... ——
Energy .... ——
Self-discipline .... ——
Perseverance .... ——
Autonomy .... ——
Assertiveness .... ——
Intelligence/related aptitudes .... ——
Leadership .... ——
Tolerance .... ——
Compassion .... ——
Perceptiveness .... ——
Spontaneity .... ——
Self-centeredness .... ——
Achievement .... ——
Kindness .... ——
Self-awareness .... ——
Loyalty/commitment .... ——
Initiative .... ——
Resourcefulness .... ——
Curiosity .... ——
Patience .... ——
Generosity .... ——
Sociability .... ——
Loneliness .... ——

Spirituality .... _____
Other: _____ _____
           _____ _____
           _____ _____

31.   What are your current interests/hobbies/leisure or recreational activities?

_____
_____
_____
_____
_____

32.   List any artistic/musical talents and/or inventions/discoveries:

_____
_____
_____
_____

33.   In this study we have worked with the notion of a legacy which has developed as a result of events and efforts in the 1960s and 70s on behalf of women. From your perspective,

    a.   What are the essential or specific elements of that legacy?

    b.   Where has that legacy fallen short in terms of present issues and needs of women?

34.   If you could put *just one item* on a list of issues or concerns which need to be addressed on behalf of women in the next 5–10 years, what would that item be?

_____

35. What percent of your *current volunteer or professional time* do you spend on what you would consider primarily on behalf of women? ___%

36. Which of the following statements most closely represents your own assessment of the past two decades of the women's movement in relation to the present situation of women in American society (circle one)? If no statement comes close, indicate how you would portray the relationship in #4 that follows.

    1—Major shifts in social, economic, and political status of women have occurred which make women's issues *per se* much less compelling than they were in the 1960s and 70s; we are about two-thirds of the way toward the goals of those early efforts.

    2—On some dimensions we have witnessed considerable progress, but there are a sufficient number of remaining issues and problems to make a 50–50 assessment more realistic.

    3—Despite some progress and considerable visibility, the real gains for women are relatively few; coupled with current backlash and other economic, political, and social factors, we have perhaps reached the one-third to halfway mark with considerable challenges ahead on behalf of women.

    4—

37. In your lifetime, what woman (or women) most fully embodies the term "leader"? Why? (If the person is not a public figure, please use some identifying characteristics, e.g., position, relationship.)

38.   At this point in your life, what is your highest priority, or your primary concern? Where are you putting your most effort or energy?

39.   In your interview we asked for names of other women you might consider *instigators* (women who initiated activities on behalf of women in the 1960s and 70s) or *inheritors* (women who have carried on the efforts begun earlier). If you have additional names to recommend, please add them here (with addresses and/or titles whenever possible).

Please feel free to provide any additional information you wish in the space provided below:

THANK YOU FOR YOUR COOPERATION

REFERENCES

Astin, H. S. "Young Women and Their Roles." In R. Havinghurst and P. Dryer (eds.), *Youth in the Seventies*. Chicago: National Society for the Study of Education, University of Chicago Press, 1975.

Bennis, W., and Nanus, B. *Leadership: The Strategies of Taking Charge*. New York: Harper & Row, 1985.

Boxer, M. J. "For and About Women: The Theory and Practice of Women's Studies in the United States." *Signs*, 1982, 7 (3), 661–695.

Brown, S. M. "Male Versus Female Leaders: A Comparison of Empirical Studies." *Sex Roles: A Journal of Research*, 1979, 5 (5), 595–611.

Carroll, S. J. "Feminist Scholarship on Political Leadership." In B. Kellerman (ed.), *Leadership: Multidisciplinary Perspectives*. Englewood Cliffs, N.J.: Prentice-Hall, 1984.

"Challenge: Women in Higher Education." Report from a Network of U.S. Office of Education Summer Institutes. University of Pittsburgh, 1972.

Erikson, E. *Identity and the Life Cycle*. New York: Norton, 1980.

Freeman, J. *The Politics of Women's Liberation*. New York: Longman, 1975.

Friedan, B. *The Feminine Mystique*. New York: Dell, 1963.

Gardner, J. W. *On Leadership.* New York: Free Press, 1990.

Guido-DiBrito, F., Carpenter, D. S., and DiBrito, W. F. "Women in Leadership and Management: Review of the Literature, 1985 Update." *NASPA Journal,* 1986, *23* (3), 22–31.

Hollander, E. P. "Leadership and Power." In G. Lindzey and E. Aronson (eds.), *Handbook of Social Psychology.* New York: Random House, 1985.

Hornig, L. S. "HERstory." *Grants Magazine,* 1978, *1* (1), 36–42.

Howe, F. "Education for Survival." In *Sex Role Stereotypes Project.* Final Report to the National Education Association, July 1973.

Kotter, J. P. *The Leadership Factor.* New York: Free Press, 1988.

Kuhn, T. S. *The Structure of Scientific Revolutions.* 2nd ed. Chicago: University of Chicago Press, 1970.

Lerner, G. "The Rise of Feminist Consciousness." In E. M. Bender, B. Burk, and N. Walker, *All of Us Are Present.* Columbia, Mo.: James Madison Wood Research Institute, Stephens College, 1984.

Morrison, A. M., White, R. P., and Van Velsor, E. *Breaking the Glass Ceiling.* Reading, Mass.: Addison-Wesley, 1987.

Nieva, V., and Gutek, B. A. *Women and Work.* New York: Praeger, 1981.

Powell, G., and Butterfield, D. A. "If 'Good Managers' Are Masculine, What Are 'Bad Managers'?" *Sex Roles: A Journal of Research,* 1984, *10* (7/8), 477–484.

Rogers, C. *Carl Rogers on Personal Power.* London: Constable, 1978.

Rossi, A. S. *Seasons of a Woman's Life.* Amherst: Social and Demographic Research Institute, University of Massachusetts, 1983.

Schwartz, F. "Catalyst at 25: Promoting the Potential of Corporate Women." Annual review Sept. 1985–Sept. 1986. New York: Catalyst, 1986.

Schwartz, F. "Review of Catalyst Capabilities." Report. New York: Catalyst, Sept. 1987.

Scott, A. F. *Making the Invisible Woman Visible.* Urbana: University of Illinois Press, 1984.

Sklar, K. K. "American Female Historians in Context, 1770-1930." *Feminist Studies,* 1975, *3* (1-2), 175–183.

Stimpson, C. R. "Gerda Lerner on the Future of Our Past." *Ms.*, Sept. 1981, pp. 51-52, 93.

Stimpson, C. R., Burstyn, J. N., Stanton, D. C., and Whisler, S. M. Editorial in *Signs*, 1975, *1* (1), pp. v-viii.

Stratton, J. "Welcoming Remarks." In J. A. Mattfeld and C. G. Van Aken (eds.), *Women and the Scientific Professions*. Cambridge, Mass.: MIT Press, 1965.

Van't Hul, N. (ed.). "1964-1984: A Report." Ann Arbor, Mich.: Center for Continuing Education of Women, University of Michigan, 1984.

INDEX

197